"Nature to be commanded must be obeyed."

Francis Bacon

THE
UNCOMMON LOON

TEXT BY TERRY McENEANEY
PHOTOGRAPHS BY MICHAEL QUINTON
FOREWORD BY FRANK C. CRAIGHEAD, JR.

 Northland Publishing

This book is dedicated to
HERB CILLEY
of Bow Lake, New Hampshire,

a fine human being, the best of loon rangers,
friend of common loons, and friend of anyone
who cares about loons.

FRONTISPIECE: *The characteristic red eyes and black and white feathers*
make the common loon one of nature's most beautiful creatures.

Text copyright ©1991 by Terry McEneaney

Photographs copyright ©1991 by Michael Quinton

Illustrations by David Jenney,

©1991 by Northland Publishing

FIRST EDITION

ISBN 0-87358-510-0

Library of Congress Catalog Card Number 90-53282

Cataloging in Publication Data

McEneaney, Terry.
The uncommon loon / text by Terry McEneaney ;
photographs by Michael Quinton.—1st ed.
128 p. cm.
Includes bibliographical references.
ISBN 0-87358-510-0 : $15.95
1. Common loon. I. Title.
QL696.G33M34 1991
598′ .442—dc20   90-53282 CIP

4/91-7.5M-0294

Contents

A Paragon of Beauty

"The loon is a paragon of beauty. Alert, supple, vigorous, one knows himself to be in the presence of the master wild thing, when he comes upon a loon on guard in his native element. The bird seems to move without effort, a single backward kick of one of those immense paddles serving to send it forward at any desired speed, while the head is turned inquiringly from side to side as if to take your measure. A short, a false motion, the flash of a gun, and the wild thing has vanished, leaving scarcely a ripple to mark its recent resting place. It reappears, if at all, at surprisingly great distance, and if really alarmed only the head is thrust out of water to take breath, get bearings, and disappear again.

"Underwater the loon moves with great rapidity using its wings [actually it uses its feet] to assist its progress. It is able, thus, easily to overtake a fish, which it transfixes by stroke of its dagger-like beak and brings to the surface for consumption. When the water is clean enough to admit of it, it is a delight to watch the air bubbles which cling to the diver in the translucent depths, like a silvery coat of mail, and which he shakes off only upon emerging at the surface again.

"In singular contrast to the loon's facility and grace in the water is its behavior upon land. Since the feet are placed so far back, it must stand nearly upright, penguin-fashion; and its walk is an awkward, shuffling performance; or else, as is more likely to be the case, the bird flounders on all fours.

"It is said not to be able to take wing from the ground at all. In rising from the water the bird humps over in agony of effort, rising only by slow stages, first by threshing the surface of the water with wings and feet, then by combined running and flying, until the feet clear at last, and the aspirant attains a proper motion. Once started, the loon's flight is swift and powerful, the wings accomplishing by rapid vibration what they lack in expanse. But the hapless act of the loon's life is that of alighting."

—W. L. DAVIS, *1923*

Foreword

Terry McEneaney and Michael Quinton have pooled their special tal-
ents and expertise to produce an interesting, highly informative book
that captures the mystique of the common loon and its wilderness environment. The lay birdwatcher seeking a first sighting of a loon as well
as the professional ornithologist concerned with annual life cycles, bird
navigation, and species distribution will find factual and original information systematically presented and beautifully illustrated.

The reader who has not seen or heard a common loon may well be
encouraged to do so—inspired by the photographs, helped by the text, and
with the assurance that loons can be found almost anywhere—but locat-
ing them depends upon a variety of factors, including season, weather
conditions, and food availability. By thus making use of the wealth of
information in this book, you will be helping to fulfill its purpose: "to
aid and add to your enjoyment of the common loon." This, in turn,
leads to a rapport with loons that automatically encourages protection.

Walking the spruce-fir shoreline of a pristine northern lake or silent-
ly cutting a swath through its dark waters, you may, from the bow of a
canoe, make your first contact with the common loon—its exciting, eerie
tremolo call coming from far across the lake. This call, a danger signal,
fills the air with sound and arouses mysterious feelings in the observer
not hitherto experienced and difficult to describe. In combination, the
beauty of the bird, the wilderness setting, and the stimulating yet haunting call make an initial impression that will never be forgotten. With today's technology, you can capture this call of the loon on tape and listen
to it at your leisure. It will remind you of enjoyable experiences with the
common loon and fuel the desire for more in the future.

*Sensing danger, a common
loon prepares to streak
across the lake (oaring) to
chase an intruder
from its nest.*

For the loon to complete its annual cycle from one egg-laying to the next, it needs separate summer and winter environments, as do many other birds. Not only must near-pristine northern hemisphere lakes be preserved, but also the southern, ice-free bodies of fresh- and saltwater. This book emphasizes the need to preserve loon habitat and suggests how this might be accomplished. It can start with you, the individual. Once you have learned about the common loon, seen it, and heard its mysterious song, you will become an admirer and active champion of this beautiful bird.

Frank C. Craighead, Jr.

Acknowledgments

No book today is written as the result of one person's efforts. A book about common loons in North America requires teamwork and cooperation. The following people have contributed to this book in one form or another and deserve to be mentioned:

Photographer Michael Quinton, for his fabulous common loon photos, friendship, comments, and input, and most importantly for asking me to team up with him to do this book. It has been a real pleasure.

Loon experts Bill Barklow, Herb Cilley, Jeff Fair, Judith McIntyre, Don Skaar, Paul Strong, Scott Sutcliffe, and Rawson Wood, who were kind enough to be interviewed for this book.

Jeff Fair, for his support and friendship and, in particular, introducing me to Herb Cilley.

Frank Craighead, Jr., for his friendship and for taking time out of his busy outdoor schedule to write the Foreword to this book.

Birders who were kind enough to give me information about common loons in their respective states, including Dan Bridges (Colorado), Charlie Clark (Texas), Dave Easterla (Missouri), and Lloyd Moore (Kansas).

Betti Arnold Albrecht and Susan McDonald of Northland Publishing for believing in me and for their editorial review of the manuscript.

My wife, Karen McEneaney, for her love of common loons, her finely illustrated plumages of common loons, and her support, ideas, patience, and understanding in completing the manuscript.

Finally, I wish to thank the unsung heroes who not only enjoy the sight and sounds of common loons, but have dedicated their time and energy to loon conservation so future generations can enjoy the common loon.

Prologue

The setting was the glacier-scarred landscape of Greenland, July 1980. To the east of me lay the huge Greenland icecap, to the west, the seacoast, and to the north, in front of me, thousands of lakes of different dimensions. Many of these lakes contained fish, primarily arctic char. Greenland is a paradise for mosquitoes, old squaws, wheatears, rock ptarmigan, gyrfalcons, peregrine falcons, and common loons.

I had traveled to Greenland to study peregrine falcons, but quickly learned the trip was much more than that. I was there with ten other biologists from the United States to find peregrine falcon eyries and determine their productivity. We were working in field teams of two individuals; I was teamed up with a very interesting character, a modern-day survivalist, a mountain man, by the name of Jack Oar. Jack and I had been assigned to a very remote area of Greenland, so we planned our trip accordingly: Jack was to carry the food, and I was to carry the camping gear. We were given a ride by boat down a fjord and began our journey.

We hiked for several hours prior to lunch. It was then I realized we were in deep trouble. I looked into Jack's backpack and asked him where the food was. He told me there was no food, that we were going to live off the land. He elaborated that he had been in Greenland before and thought we could live off the land quite comfortably. He pulled out a compact .22-calibre rifle and assured me there would be no problem.

We studied the magnificient peregrine falcon in the beautiful but hostile landscape and in our spare time made a concerted effort to secure food. Some days all we ate were arctic char, some days ptarmigan, other days berries, and some days we went entirely without food. It was us against the elements, and so far the elements had the best of us.

Adult common loon on nest.

XIV

A pair of common loons cruise their piece of wild shoreline on Stillwater Reservoir.

As the days wore on, our body weights dropped and we became more and more delirious. A live ptarmigan was quickly transfixed in one's mind as being cooked and on a platter, sort of like what you see in cartoons. We were desperate; we would eat anything to survive.

I'll never forget the day. It was 27 July 1980. We were walking along the shore of a lake, and out in the middle of this huge wind-swept lake sat a pair of common loons. Being delirious, I yelled to Jack, pointed out the loons, and demanded the rifle. I braced my body on a large boulder, held firm my arms, and took a shot at one of the loons five hundred yards out in the middle of this lake. I killed that loon, very much to my surprise, and felt absolutley terrible. The wailing calls of its mate made me feel very small. I kept talking to myself; guilt was written all over my face. In self-discussion, I told myself that since I shot it, I had better eat it. I took off my clothes and swam out to retrieve the loon. The water was incredibly cold. When I got there, I wondered how I was going to get this large bird back to shore. Quickly I realized there was only one way and like a retriever I swam to shore with the loon in my mouth. When I reached shore, I was totally exhausted and nearly hypothermic.

After warming up by a campfire, I kept asking myself what I had done. The death of this magnificent beautiful creature just tore me apart. Hunger or no hunger, I still felt terrible. I couldn't believe how beautiful that loon was, especially up close. We ate the loon that night. It took quite a while to cook. We were so hungry, we ate it almost raw. As we chewed on the meat, I asked Jack what he thought of the loon. In a quiet, low voice he replied, "You know, the worst thing I ever ate in my life was a coyote. This tastes worse than a coyote." My jaws dropped as he made his statement. I think much of that bad taste came from the guilt we felt over killing such a beautiful creature.

Introduction

There have been a number of excellent books written about the common loon (*Gavia immer*). All have something to offer, but most concentrate on common loons east of the Mississippi River and south of the Canadian/United States border. They also emphasize only one segment of the loon's life, that of nesting and chick development. This book has a much broader scope than other loon books. The emphasis here is on the common loon's physical appearance, annual life cycle, distribution—which encompasses all of North America and sections of the northern hemisphere—and future.

The common loon is revered by many people as being one of the most majestic birds in North America. Its reputation for grandeur is based on strikingly simple yet beautifully arranged black and white feathers characteristic of an adult in breeding plumage. In Europe, this same bird is called the Great Northern Diver. This book focuses on North America, where the bird is primarily distributed and the name common loon is used to describe this feathered model of uncommon beauty.

Besides the beautiful plumage, the common loon is noted for its diving ability and its incredible vocalizations. The sounds made by this bird bring chills to the spine, for few sounds in nature equal the tremolo, wail, and yodel calls that characterize the common loon. The common loon is one of the few birds that we directly associate with a particular type of habitat, whether we actually see them or only hear them calling, for the graceful loon represents the quality we are seeking in a wilderness experience. The call of the loon conjures images of remote, peaceful lakes and is therefore associated with wilderness or wild places. However, not all northern lakes where loons nest are truly isolated and remote; some have large numbers of people, yet common loons can exist on these lakes as long as there is an adequate supply of food and undisturbed areas where they can rest, nest, and rear their young.

Loons need open water in order to take off; they get a "running" start by oaring with their webbed feet.

1

The word "common" means of ordinary occurrence or appearance. Common loons can be found almost anywhere in North America, but the key is to know when and where to look for them. All loons migrate to some extent, some farther than others. Migrant loons can be found almost anywhere there is suitable habitat, that is, undisturbed shallow water areas where there is an abundance of small fish. They can be found in areas you least expect them, such as the deserts of Arizona, California, Nevada, New Mexico, Texas, and Utah. Common loons have been known to migrate through the driest and hottest country in North America, such as the Mohave Desert and Death Valley. Excellent areas to watch large numbers of migrant common loons include Whitefish Point (Michigan), Long Point (Ontario), Pigeon Point (California), Point Judith (Rhode Island), and Hawk Mountain (Pennsylvania), to name a few. There is much to be learned about common loons but one thing is certain, they are more ordinarily occurring than people think.

The story of the common loon is a tale not only of two distinct plumages, but of two distinct habitat types. The common loon trans-forms from a bird of strikingly beautiful plumage in the summer to a dull-colored plumage characteristic of winter. The habitats also change dramatically from clear freshwater lakes in the northern latitudes where they nest in the summer to saltwater coasts where they winter. Fresh-water inland lakes can also be occupied by loons in the winter but is dependent on mild winter weather conditions. The habitat a loon chooses in the winter varies anywhere from large ice-free inland lakes and rivers to brackish estuaries, saltwater coasts, and shallow seas.

Common loons are not easily detected on the wintering areas, because they rarely vocalize and have relatively dull-colored plumage. From January to as late as March, loons go through a flightless period in which they synchronously molt their flight feathers. For many peo-ple, common loons are difficult to identify when they are in this drab winter or basic plumage.

The common loon is our link to the environment. The calls of the common loon are truly reminiscent of a wilderness concerto. This one avian species stands out in bold relief against nature's complex orchestra of sounds. Common loons are the epitome of a quality environment. Their welfare is dependent upon an entire web of ecological relationships with other life forms since they are at the top of the aquatic food chain—they are feathered "environmental monadnocks." These exquisite birds stand out by themselves and their mere presence on a lake keeps us abreast of the state of our environment. People can make a difference, and as long as there are dedicated people and organizations working toward a common goal we will have loons for many generations to come. I sincerely hope that the words and photographs found in this book will aid and add to your enjoyment of the common loon.

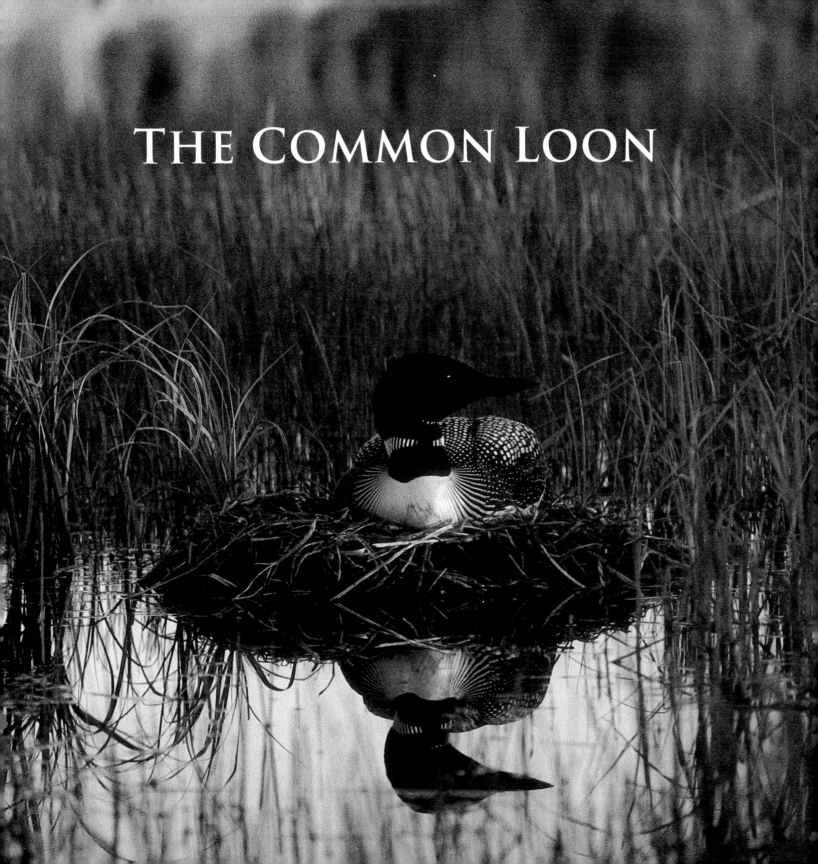

THE COMMON LOON

Loons in General

Loons, also known as divers, are large, primarily fish-eating, diving birds inhabiting fresh- and saltwater habitats of the northen hemisphere. On water, they are easily recognizable by their low silhouettes, sleek compact bodies, short tails, thick necks, and daggerlike bills. In flight, loons have efficient streamlined bodies with a characteristic hunchback profile, the head slightly lower than the body. Loons have remarkably small wings for such large-bodied birds and have very rapid wingbeats, resulting in fast speed and maximizing the loon's ability to stay airborne.

Opposite: The average common loon is one and a half times the size of a mallard but much more streamlined in appearance.

Loons all belong to the single genus *Gavia,* which contains five species: the common loon *(G. immer),* the yellow-billed loon or great northern diver *(G. adamsii),* the Pacific loon *(G. pacifica),* the Arctic loon *(G. arctica),* and the red-throated loon *(G. stellata).* All five species can be found in North America. Key characteristics used in identifying these species include bill size, shape, profile, and color; head shape, profile, and color; body size, shape, and color; habitat; and behavior. Common and yellow-billed loons, for example, are unique in that they dive by sliding under the surface of the water, whereas the other three loon species hop slightly upward and forward before initiating the dive.

Physical Appearance

The common loon is a large bird measuring twenty-four to thirty-six inches in length, weighing from eight to thirteen pounds, and having a wingspan of up to fifty-eight inches. The average common loon weighs between eight and ten pounds. For comparative purposes, the common loon is basically one and a half times the size of a mallard but much more streamlined in appearance.

The bill of the common loon is long, daggerlike, and compressed on the sides, uniquely adapted for taking fish under the surface of the water. The large head has a steep-sloped forehead and an obvious crown that is supported by a thick neck (Figure 1). The length of the bill increases with age: juveniles characteristically have short thick bills, whereas adults have long thin bills (Figure 2). Bill color also varies with age and time of the year. Adults in spring and summer have shiny black bills, whereas in winter both adults and juveniles have dull gray bills. The nostrils, located on the bill, have a movable flap that closes when the loon dives. The neck and jaw muscles of the loon are strong and adapted for jabbing fish or for manipulating nest material. Fish are typically captured with the tip of the bill, primarily through a lightning fast puncture strike, but can also be caught between the vise-like mandibles. Typical of most birds, the mandibles look rigid but are actually flexible, particularly near the base of the skull.

Figure 1.
Physical characteristics of a common loon.

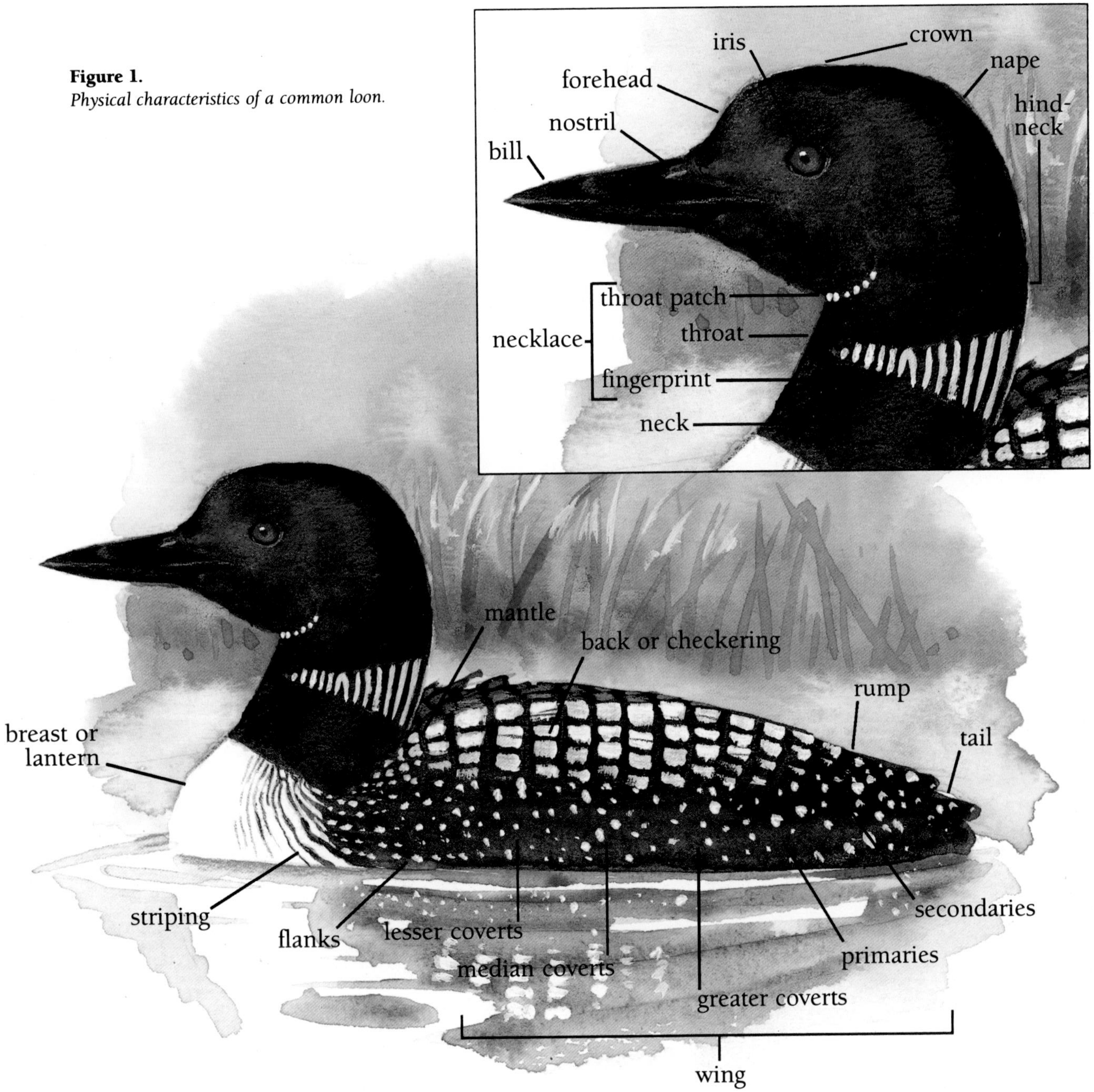

THE MYSTERIOUS FISH KILL

One May day, Mike Quinton visited Twin Lakes in Idaho and watched migrant loons congregate on their spring staging area. There were over one hundred common loons on these two connected reservoirs at the time. Typical daily loon behavior involved breaking up into small feeding territories by day and rafting in large groups at night. One amusing point of interest was the difficulty these loons had in swallowing what was believed to be bluegills. One by one they would surface with the prey, but had some difficulty swallowing the fish.

On this particular day, a wind storm suddenly appeared with gusts in excess of seventy miles per hour. The loons were forced to leave their feeding areas by taking off into the wind; but the force of the wind was so strong that as soon as the loons attempted to take off, they would crash-land nearly vertically into the water. They eventually congregated into one large raft on the lee side of the lake.

After the windstorm, Mike found dozens of fish floating belly-up on the sand beach along the south shore of the lake. Upon closer examination, he discovered that each fish had puncture holes on the throat that resembled marks made by tin snips. The only explanation he could come up with was that they had been killed by loons but the loons had not been able to swallow them. The windstorm had washed them ashore.

adult

6 weeks

4 weeks

1 week

Figure 2. *Development of the common loon's eyes and bill.*

Ingestion of small prey characteristically occurs underwater. Diving loons normally surface to get oxygen before swallowing the food. Large prey is often thrown slightly in the air and then quickly swallowed in one gulp. Sometimes there are problems with large prey, in which case the loon will reposition the fish on the water surface before it is swallowed. Loons typically swallow their prey head-first, however, not all prey captured is consumed. On several occasions, I have watched common loons trying to swallow very large prey. In such cases they jab at the fish and attempt to swallow it, only to cough it up. After numerous attempts at swallowing the prey, the loons give up, leaving the fish floating on the surface of the water. These fish are never wasted, however, and are quickly consumed by scavengers.

The eyes of the loon, like all birds, are fixed in sockets. Although restricted in movement, the eyes are counterbalanced through the aid of the loon's long flexible neck. Only the pupil and colored iris are visible; the remainder of the eye is concealed behind movable eyelids made of skin. A somewhat hidden nictitating membrane (think of this as an inner eyelid) is located in front of the eye and moves quickly and occasionally across the eye surface to cleanse and protect the eye. The color of the eyes changes with the age of the loon. The iris is dark brown when a chick hatches and quickly changes to yellow-brown, then to brown-red when the chick is several weeks old, and eventually turns to bright red when the loon is an adult (Figure 2).

The characteristic bright red eye of an adult common loon helps the bird search for prey underwater by filtering out yellow, orange, and red light and absorbing blue and violet light.

The red eyes typically found in adult loons are the result of a combination of oil droplets, pigments, and reflected red light. A color is created by an impulse of light of a differing wave length. The red eyes act very similar to water in that they both filter out light in the upper end of the light spectrum (yellow, orange, and red), and absorb light in the lower end of the spectrum (blue and violet). Loons are therefore at an advantage when they dive for prey because they not only see prey easily underwater, but prey have a difficult time seeing loons underwater. The red eye is difficult to see underwater, especially the deeper a loon dives, due to the reduction in light from the upper end of the light spectrum.

The legs and feet of the common loon are strong, designed for propulsion and diving. Loon bones are thick, solid, and heavy, uniquely adapted for diving. The long legs are positioned near the rear of the body, which allows the feet to act like oars, thus maximizing power diving. The femur, or thigh, is short and encased under the feathered skin. The legs are black or blackish on the outside and light blue-gray on the inside. The webbed feet are black or blackish below and light blue-gray above with toenails that are flat. The feet are used for swimming and preening those parts of the body that can't be reached with the bill, primarily the head. They are also used for takeoffs, which the loon begins by facing into the wind and running across the surface of the water, flapping its wings to get airborne. Due to the position of the legs on the body, the common loon moves poorly on land. It makes small hops that start with thrusts from the legs and wings and end by landing on the breast—the movement resembles someone on crutches.

The loon's feet are used for takeoffs, which the loon begins by facing into the wind and running across the surface of the water, flapping its wings to get airborne.

The common loon is a bird of stark contrast due to its beautiful black and white pattern. The plumage most easily recognizable is that of an adult in summer plumage. The male loon is almost indistinguishable from the female: the male is slightly larger and is the only member of a mated pair to yodel. The head of an adult loon appears to be black, but with proper light conditions will shine a typical glossy, velvety greenish black or sometimes a lustrous iridescent purple, depending on the angle of the light. The necklace of the common loon is a series of sharply defined white vertical streaks, either independent of one another or connected, positioned in two places below the throat (throat patch) and on either side of the neck (Figures 1 and 4a). The necklace is one of a kind on each loon and is the equivalent of a human fingerprint. Individual birds can be identified by their necklace configuration. The lower breast of the common loon is pure white and is sometimes referred to as the lantern. On each side of the breast are curved black and white stripes, appropriately called striping.

The remaining part of the body that can be seen above water is basically black with sharply defined white spots located on the back, scapulars ("shoulders"), mantle (back, scapulars, wings), sides, and flanks. All tail, upper tail coverts, and flight feathers are entirely black. The most striking feathers on the large body are those located on the back and scapulars. Each of these black contour feathers has two white spots; the white pattern can vary from square or rectangular to oval, depending on the location. It is this area of the back that gives the common loon its characteristic checkered pattern.

In contrast to the remarkably beautiful upper body plumage, the underparts of the common loon are relatively simple in general appearance. The underparts—breast, belly, underwing coverts, wings, and vent feathers—are white year-round, even on immature loons.

Fall and winter plumage are totally different than spring and summer plumage. Adults in fall plumage undergo a feather molt change that is most noticeable in the breast, back, and head areas (Figure 4b). The striping on the sides of the breast begins to be replaced by white feathers. The same is true for the area around the throat, chin, neck, eye, and back. The black feathers are replaced by white feathers at this time of the year, creating a ragged, mottled appearance.

An adult in winter plumage.

Adults in winter plumage are basically gray in general appearance. On the back and scapulars, the square-tipped feathers change to a gray color with very faint spots or rectangles barely noticeable unless viewed up close. The throat, chin, neck, breast, and other underparts are white. There are areas of dark plumage that characterize adult winter plumage: dark gray on the hind neck, which extends around the front portions of the neck giving it a half-collar appearance; and that area of the head called the nape. In both cases, the nape and hind neck are darker than the back (Figure 4c). The bill and the feet are lighter in color in the winter than in the summer, and the lower mandible and parts of the upper mandible are an ivory gray color in winter.

Plumage also varies according to age. Young loons in first winter plumage are similar to adults in winter plumage, but the most noticeable difference is the short, thick bill characteristic of younger loons (Figure 2). The bill is light gray in color and is slightly darker only on the ridges. The key characteristic of a juvenile in winter plumage is the overall brown-gray body color and scaled appearance of the feathers on the back, mantle, and scapulars (Figure 3 and 4d).

These scaled feathers are round-tipped, as opposed to the usual square-tipped feathers found in adults (Figure 3). The back, nape, and hind-neck are dark gray-brown in color, and only the back differs due to the scaled appearance of the feathers.

Newly hatched loon chicks are born completely covered with black down, with the exception of the belly, which is white. After the first week, the black down is replaced by a second series of down feathers, which are brown-gray in color. As the chicks grow older, these feathers fade and the chicks appear to be a combination of brown and gray. After several weeks, the chicks are mostly gray with some brown inter-mixed and have the characteristic scaled feathers that typify the juvenile common loon.

Figure 3. *Round-tipped juvenile feathers vs. square-tipped adult feathers.*

Newly hatched loon chicks are covered with down until they are several weeks old.

a   b

c   d

Figure 4. *The changing appearance of a common loon:*
a) adult in summer, or breeding, plumage; b) adult in fall plumage
c) adult in winter plumage; d) juvenile in winter plumage.

THE SILVER BULLET

Every summer I travel to a lake and make a specific trip just to check on a pair of nesting common loons. I usually travel to this area by boat and make it a point to be as quiet as possible, especially when nearing the nest. It is sort of a ritual for me. As I approach a particular point on the lake, I softly paddle along the shoreline and spot what appears to be a gray rock to the unaided eye, but with binoculars is clearly identified as an incubating adult loon with the head held very low and close to the water's edge. I usually paddle ever so slightly toward the loon, and the loon sinks into the water like a snake, barely making a wake in the water.

Then I search the clear water for the swimming loon. Sure enough there it is, the silver bullet, with air bubbles clinging to its feathers, passing right underneath the boat. The silver bullet is a personal experience that only occurs for four seconds every year, but for me, it is the thrill of a lifetime. The adult loon surfaces forty yards from my boat and makes the tremolo call. This is my signal to leave the area, so I quickly look at the nest from the boat and count the eggs through my binoculars, then paddle out to the middle of the lake and do not feel comfortable until the adult returns to the nest—my actions could affect the outcome of incubation. The adult loon returns to the nest, and I head out. As I paddle back across the lake, I relish the memory of the silver bullet swimming underneath my boat. A four-second experience has left an indelible mark on my mind.

Wilderness Concerto

To many people the common loon is a symbol of wilderness, more closely associated with it than the wolf or the grizzly bear. Common loons represent the quality that people are seeking in wilderness.

The wildness associated with loons is a function of their habitat, their unique repertoire of calls, and the sheer mysterious nature of loons in general. Prime summer loon habitat must be quality habitat— that is, it must have clean, fresh, clear lake water with an abundance of quality food, which in most cases is fish, but in some rare instances may include leeches, insects, and even amphibians.

Spruce-fir forests are the most common plant communities surrounding these lake habitats, although the vegetation does not totally identify areas where common loons are known to nest. In Greenland, for example, common loons nest on lakes created by glaciers so there are no trees surrounding the lakes; instead, the lakes are surrounded by low-growing sedges, cottongrass, granite boulders, and granite cliffs. In parts of Maine and New Hampshire, characteristic lake habitat includes deciduous trees such as maple and oak. In parts of northern Minnesota, lakes are bordered by spruce and fir; in Yellowstone National Park, located in northern Wyoming, the lakes are bordered by lodgepole pine. Regardless of the vegetative habitat surrounding a lake, the most important element is solitude. It is these quality lakes with an abundance of food that loons seek out for nesting.

Common loon habitat is three dimensional: it involves length, width, and depth. In the summer, common loon habitat also involves three levels of space, almost like little worlds in themselves, which include the sky, or air, the surface of the water, and underwater. The air is used for quick transportation and movement from one area to another. Flying around in the air is a way of communicating. Loons also fly when agitated or disturbed and circle the territory notifying the mate (and in some cases

Prime summer habitat for common loons must include clean, fresh lake water and an abundance of quality food—usually fish. Pictured is Stillwater Reservoir, New York.

other loons) with a tremolo call that an intruder is in the area.

The surface of the water is where we typically see common loons. A variety of activities occur here, including preening, sleeping, swallowing prey, wing-stretching, calling, courtship, aggressive displays, and parental care of the young. The surface of the water can be more than just two dimensional, such as we encounter on calm days; it becomes three dimensional when wind and waves enter the picture.

The underwater world of the common loon is the area about which we know the least, yet a large amount of a loon's time is spent underwater. Although loons typically dive for less than a minute at a time, they still spend a lot of time underwater each day because of the frequency of dives. Common loons defend underwater territories as well as surface territories and may chase intruders underwater, where they move extremely fast and can cover tremendous distances. Loons typically search shallow areas for prey since small fishes hide in these areas where the amount of escape cover (debris, rocks, lily pads, reeds) is greater. The shallower the water the more complex the lake bottom, thus allowing small fish a greater chance of survival. The deeper one follows the lake bottom the less complex it becomes, and oftentimes all that is found in deep water are relatively flat lake bottoms with thick layers of suspended sediments. Small fishes have a difficult time surviving at these depths due to the lack of food and escape cover. Underwater, common loons scan large areas of water every time they dive, quickly maneuvering around obstacles that typically hide small fish. Since loons must travel faster than fish in order to catch them, they have greater success catching the slow-moving fish. Fast-moving fish such as trout and salmon are harder to catch but present no problem where large numbers of fish are available.

Adult and newly hatched chick from underwater.

Loon Calls

There are numerous unique wild sounds in this world, such as the howling of the wolf or the laughing of the hyena. But few can compare with the sounds made by the common loon. We refer to the loon's call as the symbol of the wilderness, but it represents a unique repertoire of calls. The different calls have entirely different meanings; only in recent years have these meanings been understood to some degree, thanks to the pioneering work of William Barklow of Framingham State College in Massachusetts. He ascertained that loons call primarily at night and that their calls can be categorized into four basic sounds: wails, tremolos, yodels, and hoots. The familiar wolflike wail is perhaps the most frequently heard of all the loon calls. The wail is used to summon a mate or contact a chick. The laughing tremolo is used to signal alarm, usually due to a disturbance in the territory by an intruder such as another loon, a predator, or people. It is the tremolo, the maniacal laugh, that is undoubtedly responsible for the cliché, "crazy as a loon." The yodel, on the other hand, is performed exclusively by the male loon and is actually a song. It is used in defense and identification of a territory. Individual male loons can be identified by their unique yodel, which is a form of vocal fingerprinting. The hoot, or "kwuk," is a one-syllable call with a variety of pitches and is used to maintain contact between mated loon pairs and their chicks. Few species can compete with the wild concerto calls of the common loon.

The yodel is performed exclusively by the male and is actually a song.

HABITAT & DISTRIBUTION

Nesting and Summer Distribution

The common loon inhabits only the northern hemisphere, with primary concentration occurring in northern North America. Nesting distribution of the common loon in North America encompasses northeast Washington; northern and northeast Idaho; western Montana; northeast Wyoming; northeast North Dakota; northern Minnesota; northern Wisconsin; northern and central Michigan; northeast New York; northern Massachusetts; Vermont; New Hampshire; Maine; New Brunswick; Nova Scotia; Prince Edward Island; Newfoundland; southern Baffin Island; Quebec; Ontario; Manitoba; southeast, central, and northern Saskatchewan; central and northern Alberta; British Columbia; southern Northwest Territories; Yukon Territory; and Alaska (Figure 5). Summer distribution also includes eastern, southern, and western Greenland; Iceland; and Bear Island (Bjornoya). Small numbers of nonbreeding common loons have been reported on the Komandorskiye Ostrova (Commander Islands, U.S.S.R.), Faroe Islands, and Spitsbergen Islands.

Opposite: Lily pad lakes provide plenty of clean, fresh water for nesting loons but are often without fish.

Common loons prefer to nest on isolated lakes with shallow water areas for securing food, building nests, and rearing young. Emergent vegetation in these shallow water areas or thick plantlife along the shoreline are sought out by nesting loons as places for nest sites.

Not all loons nest in the summer. Subadults, nonbreeders, and some immatures either remain in the winter habitat along the coast or travel long distances and gather in small loose flocks on large lakes and reservoirs in the interior of the continent. Large interior lakes like Yellowstone Lake in Wyoming and Canyon Ferry Reservoir in Montana are examples of interior lakes where immature and subadult common loons have been observed in the summer. Immature loons are more restricted in their movements and typically remain on the coast for two to four years before attempting the spring migration.

CONFUSED BY THE SMOKE

One of the most interesting experiences I have ever had with common loons occurred during the 1988 Yellowstone wildfires. I received a call from park ranger Debbie Bird concerning an adult common loon that was stranded on a dry sewage lagoon at Old Faithful. The loon had apparently become confused and disoriented with the incredibly thick smoke and landed on the dry sewage lagoon mistaking it for water. Some park maintenance people figured out a creative way of hooking up a garden hose and ran water to the dry lagoon. When we arrived, the loon was sitting under the water spray in the moist mud. I picked up the adult loon, placed it in a cardboard box, and brought it home.

I wanted to keep it overnight, since we were losing daylight and I needed a chance to make sure the loon was not hurt. My wife, Karen, turned on the water in the bathtub, and we gave the loon the water test. The loon immediately began preening and swimmimg around the tub. I then introduced it to a common loon decoy that I happened to have, and it began making the wailing call in my bathtub. I won't get into the messy details of what happened to the bathroom, but the most important thing is that the loon was fine. The next morning I placed the loon, which I named Old Faithful, back in the cardboard box, picked up my boss at the office, and hurriedly released the loon in Mary Bay on Yellowstone Lake. There was nothing wrong with the loon. The reason it couldn't fly was that it needed water to take off. I figured Yellowstone Lake was big enough, even for a loon takeoff.

Migration and Winter Distribution

Migration is the periodic movement of a species from one region to another for feeding or breeding. These can be long- or short-distance movements, depending on the area of origin. Common loons are forced to migrate in the fall due to the weather, which severely reduces or eliminates their food supply. In the spring, the driving forces behind migration are hunger and the urge to breed. Loons migrate during the day, with most activity occurring the first four hours after sunrise. The speed with which these birds migrate varies and depends on altitude, wind speed, and wind direction. Migrant loons have been known to travel at speeds between twenty-five and one hundred miles per hour; more typically they travel at speeds between fifty and sixty miles per hour. Altitudes at which loons migrate also vary. They have been known to migrate through some of the lowest areas in North America, such as Death Valley, California, actually below sea level. More typically, however, loons migrate at ranges as low as 150 feet when over water or in excess of nine thousand feet when crossing mountain passes. On the average, they migrate within two thousand feet of the ground.

Weather plays an important role in the survival of loons during migration. In the fall, loons are forced to leave an area due to lakes freezing over: they sometimes freeze to the ice, thereby becoming vulnerable to predators. One fall in Yellowstone National Park, I watched a bald eagle kill and rip apart a live common loon that was frozen to the ice on Yellowstone Lake. Remnants of the loon carcass were later cleaned up by common ravens and coyotes. Nothing went to waste.

Loons are forced to migrate in the fall because of the weather and the subsequent reduction in food; in spring, the driving forces behind migration are hunger and the urge to breed.

During migration, common loons can be found almost anywhere. Whether or not they survive their journey depends on weather conditions. Heavy rain, snow, or fog can confuse loons and will often force them to land in unexpected places. It is not unusual to find migrant loons in gravel pits, along highways. or on wet paved parking lots and roads. I have seen loons land in sewer treatment ponds, both the wet and dry variety. Adverse weather conditions are the primary causes of loon mortality due to collisions. Under snowy or foggy conditions, power lines, fence lines, and radio tower guy wires can take their toll on migrating birds. Loons have been known to collide with masts of ships and trees, as have ducks and swans.

Rafts of common loons congregate in staging areas, where they wait, especially in spring, for the ice to break up farther north.

Common loons use both corridors and overland routes when migrating. The migratory corridors are similar to the pathways used by other waterfowl (Figure 6). In the northeastern United States, two principal corridors are used by common loons: one close to shore, paralleling the Atlantic coast, and crossing land at the peninsula of Cape Cod between Cape Cod Bay and Buzzards Bay; and the other well offshore, following the continental shelf from Maine to South Carolina. Other important corridors used by loons and waterfowl include the Great Lakes/Chesapeake Bay corridor, the Appalachian/Piedmont Plateau corridor, the Great Lakes/Mississippi River delta corridor, the northern Alberta/Texas coast corridor, and the Pacific coast corridor. The migration of birds to and from Baffin Island/Greenland and Iceland/mainland Europe remains poorly understood.

During migration, loons congregate on certain lakes or coastal bays known as staging areas where they wait, especially in the spring, for the ice to break up farther north. There are staging areas along most migratory routes, such as the Great Lakes region, Flaming Gorge Reservoir in Wyoming, Flathead Lake in Montana, and Twin Lakes in Idaho, and near coastal areas as well, such as those at the Straits of Juan de Fuca,

The arrival of adult territorial loons on a lake is closely related to ice conditions.

the Straits of Georgia, the Inland Passage, Cook Inlet on the Pacific coast of North America, and the Bay of Fundy and the Gulf of St. Lawrence on the Atlantic coast. As the ice breaks up on the northern lakes, loons spread northward and again concentrate in smaller numbers in satellite staging areas. They usually fly over the nesting territory periodically and are ready to occupy the lake once it has a fair amount of open water. The arrival of adult territorial loons on a lake is closely related to the ice conditions.

Common loon spring migration is much more hurried, concentrated, and timely compared with the fall migration, which is slower, less concentrated, and spread out over a longer period of time. Loon migration in the fall is very gradual. Fall migration normally occurs from September through December, while spring migration occurs primarily from late March through late May. Loons travel alone or in groups varying from two to fifteen individuals and in flight migrate in very small, loose groups. Adult loons are the first to migrate south and can precede immatures by as much as two to three weeks. Not all loons migrate to the coast; some overwinter on inland lakes. This is especially true during mild winters in the Great Lakes region or other areas of the continent's interior.

Loons migrate to wintering areas for two primary reasons: to secure food and to molt. On the wintering area, the common loon goes through a dramatic plumage change and loses its bright beautiful feathers, which are replaced by dull gray feathers. They remain on these wintering areas for five to six months. From late January to early March, the most significant event is the remigial molt; in other words, all flight feathers are molted, or shed, at the same time, leaving a loon completely flightless. Loons are therefore relatively sedentary during this period and remain in the immediate area. Loons do not vocalize much while on the wintering area.

Loons winter primarily on coastal waters (Figure 6); they are not often found in pelagic areas. The wintering habitat is as diverse as the summer habitat: for example, marine life in the Bay of Fundy (Canada) is quite different from the marine life found near the Florida Keys; the same can be said of the Pacific coast, where the marine life differs significantly from the Gulf of Alaska to the coast of southern California and northern Baja Mexico. It should be noted that common loons also winter along the west coast of Europe, with the typical range extending from northern Norway to southern Portugal and including the coast of the British Isles.

Loons are inland nesters that have to migrate to the coast to spend the winter. How can loons adapt to the heavy concentrations of salt found in saltwater? They secrete the excess salt through large salt glands located above the eyes on each side of the skull. It is through these supraorbital glands that salt is reduced and filtered, thereby limiting salt concentrations in the blood.

Loons frequent shallow water areas three to fifteen feet deep in search of food, whereas they will venture into deeper water, fifteen to thirty feet deep, when preening or resting. Loons have been known to dive to depths that exceed two hundred feet, but this is more the exception than the rule. Because the habitat differs from area to area, the food habits of wintering loons are quite diverse and include such prey items as rock cod, flounder, sea trout, herring, surf fish, killifish, menhoden, sculpin, crabs, and shrimp. Winter prey can also include freshwater fish if loons happen to winter in the interior of the continent.

The story of the common loon is a tale of two distinct plumages and two distinct habitats. The loon transforms from a bird of striking beauty in the summer to a dull-colored, ordinary-looking bird in the winter. The habitats also change dramatically from clear freshwater lakes in the northern latitudes during summer to saltwater coasts in the winter. Freshwater inland lakes can also be occupied by loons in the winter, but this depends on mild weather conditions. The habitat a loon chooses during migration varies anywhere from large ice-free inland lakes and rivers, to brackish estuaries, saltwater coasts, and shallow seas.

A loon flaps, part of its grooming process as well as a territorial defensive display.

A LOON IN MY BACKYARD

You don't have to go far to find a common loon. I discovered this when I lived on Red Rock Lakes National Wildlife Refuge in Montana in 1985. I was employed as a wildlife biologist, and my wife and I lived on the refuge in a house with an outstanding view a fair distance from the open water areas.

On this particular morning, I rose about 6:00 to a heavy blanket of snow and a rising thermometer. The fog was exceptionally thick as I stepped outside, and I could hear tundra swans calling as they circled overhead in confusion. At 9:00 the fog started to clear, and I noticed my next door neighbor's horse, with its ears straight up, staring at something in my backyard. I reached for my binoculars and looked at the object; sure enough it was a loon on the ground. I immediately put on my boots and walked over to the area I had last seen the loon. There it was, a common loon calling in my backyard. It was laying in the snow with a broken wing. I retraced the tracks made by the loon and quickly realized it had been injured in a collision with the powerline, which it could not see because of the fog. I wondered what might have attracted the loon across the broad wide open valley to this area. After all it seemed like an unlikely place to find a loon. I soon realized the street light had been responsible for luring the bird. Confused in the fog, the migrant loon was attracted to the light, mistaking it for the sun.

Where to See a Common Loon

Common loons can be found almost anywhere in North America, but the key is to know when and where to look for them. Nesting loons are found in northern North America in the summer (Figure 5). Migrant loons can be found almost anywhere there is suitable habitat (Figure 6). They can be found in areas you least expect them, such as the deserts of Arizona, California, Nevada, New Mexico, Texas, and Utah. Common loons have been known to migrate through the driest and hottest areas of North America—the Mojave Desert and Death Valley. Wintering loons are typically found along the coastline (Figure 6), but can be found on inland lakes, especially during mild winters.

The following information should be helpful for those interested in common loons in a particular area, and offers some suggestions as to where to look for loons.

A loon settles down to keep the eggs warm.

48

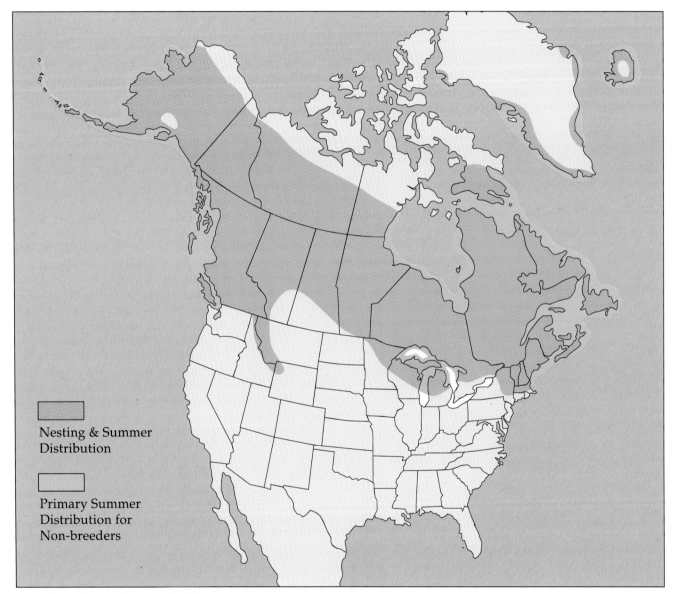

Figure 5. Nesting and Summer Distribution.

Nesting & Summer
Distribution

Primary Summer
Distribution for
Non-breeders

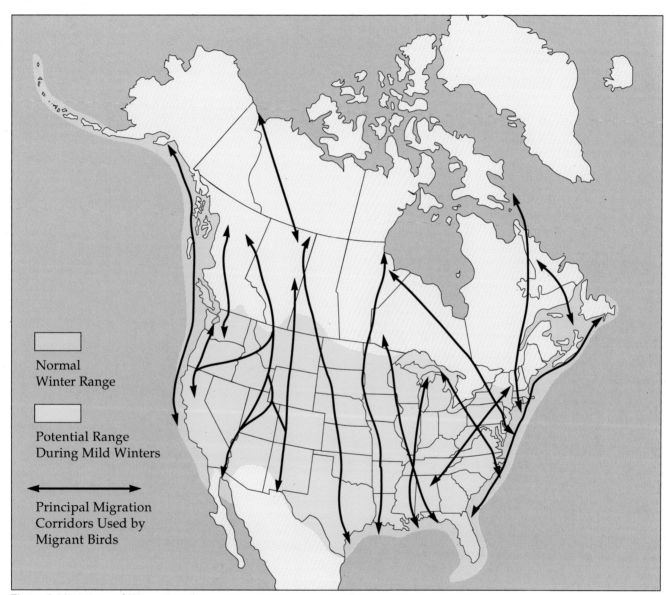

Figure 6. Migration and Winter Distribution.

Normal
Winter Range

Potential Range
During Mild Winters

Principal Migration
Corridors Used by
Migrant Birds

Eastern United States

New England /
Mid Atlantic Area

Southeast Area

Great Lakes Area

NEW ENGLAND/MIDDLE ATLANTIC AREA

State	Best Month(s)	Location
Maine	Apr.–Sept.	1 Moosehead Lake
	Apr.–Sept.	2 Sebago Lake
	Apr.–Sept.	3 Rangeley Lake
	Oct.–Mar.	4 Acadia National Park
	Oct.–Apr.	5 Cape Elizabeth
	Oct.–Mar.	6 Neck-Pine Pt. Narrows
New Hampshire	Apr.–Sept.	7 Lake Winnepesaukee
	Apr.–Sept.	8 Squam Lake
	Apr.–Sept.	9 Great East Lake
	Oct.–Mar.	10 Hampton Beach
	Oct.–Mar.	11 Rye
Vermont	May & Oct.	12 Lake Champlain
	May & Oct.	13 Lake Memphramagog
Massachusetts	Apr–Oct.	14 Quabbin Res.
	Oct.–Mar.	15 Nantucket Island
	Oct.–Mar.	16 Martha's Vineyard
	Oct.–Mar.	17 Manomet Point
	Oct.–May	18 Halibut Pt./Andrews Pt.
	Oct.–May	19 Buzzards Bay
Rhode Island	late Apr.–mid May	20 Point Judith
	Oct.–May	21 Sakonnet Pt.
	Oct.–Apr.	22 Weekapaug Beach
Connecticut	Oct.–May	23 Hammonasset Point
	Oct.–May	24 Todd's Pt./Greenwich Pt.
New York	Apr.–Sept.	25 Adirondack Park
	May & Oct.	26 Finger Lakes region
	May & Oct.	27 Rochester
	Oct.–Mar.	28 Montauk Point (Long Island)
New Jersey	Apr.	29 Culvers Lake
	Dec.–Mar.	30 Long Beach Island
	Nov.–Mar.	31 Cape May
Pennsylvania	May	32 Bald Eagle State Park
	Oct., Nov., Apr.	33 Hawk Mountain
	Oct., Nov., Apr.	34 Tuscarora Mtn. hawk lookout
	Apr.	35 Lake Marburg
Delaware	Nov.–Mar.	36 Cape Henlopen State Park
	Nov.–Mar.	37 Delaware Seashore St. Park
Maryland	Nov.–Mar.	38 Assateague/Chincoteague
	Nov.–Mar.	39 Calvert
	Oct.–Mar.	40 Sandy Point State Park
West Virginia	Apr. & Oct.	41 Cheat Lake
Virginia	Oct.–Apr.	42 Cape Charles
	Mar.	43 Matthews
	Nov. & Apr.	44 Lake Anna

SOUTHEAST AREA

State	Best Month(s)	Location
North Carolina	Nov.–Mar.	45 Pea Island NWR/Cape Hatteras
	Nov.–Mar.	46 Cape Lookout
	Nov.–Mar.	47 Fort Fisher
	Nov. & Apr.	48 Jordan Lake
South Carolina	early March	49 Kiawah Island
	Nov & Mar.	50 Lake Moultrie
	Nov.–Mar.	51 Cape Romain NWR
	Nov.–Mar.	52 Lake Hartwell
	Nov.–Mar.	53 Myrtle Beach
Georgia	late Apr.	54 Lake Lanier
	Nov.	55 Clark Hill Reservoir
	Nov.–Mar.	56 Tybee Lighthouse
	Nov.–Mar.	57 St. Simons Island (Sea Island)
Florida	Nov.–Mar.	58 Pensacola Bay
	Dec.	59 Palma Sola Bay
	Nov.–Mar.	60 Cape Canaveral/Merritt Island
Tennessee	Sept.–Apr.	61 Ft. Loudoun Lake
	Sept.–Apr.	62 Booker T. Washington State Park
	Nov.	63 Tullahoma
	Oct.–Apr.	64 Chickamauga Lake
Mississippi	Nov.–Apr.	65 Gulf Islands Nat. Seashore
	Nov.–Apr.	66 Ross Barnett Reservoir
	Nov.–Apr.	67 Gulfpoint
Alabama	Nov.–Apr.	68 Wheeler NWR
	Nov.–Apr.	69 Mobile Bay

GREAT LAKES AREA

State	Best Month(s)	Location
Ohio	Nov. & Apr.	70 Alum Creek Reservoir
	Nov. & Apr.	71 Cleveland
	Nov. & Apr.	72 Meldahl Dam
Michigan	April–mid May	73 Whitefish Point
	May–Sept.	74 Isle Royale Nat. Park
	May–Sept.	75 Seney NWR
	May–Sept.	76 western Upper Peninsula
	Nov.	77 St. Joseph
Indiana	Apr.	78 Lake Lemon
Kentucky	Apr. & Nov.	79 Dale Hollow St. Park
Illinois	Apr., May, Sept.	80 Pittsburg Lake
	Apr. & Nov.	81 Starved Rock St. Park
	Mar., Apr., Oct., Nov.	82 Chicago
Wisconsin	Oct., Nov.	83 Lake Mendota
	Apr.–Sept.	84 northern Wisconsin

Central & Western United States

52

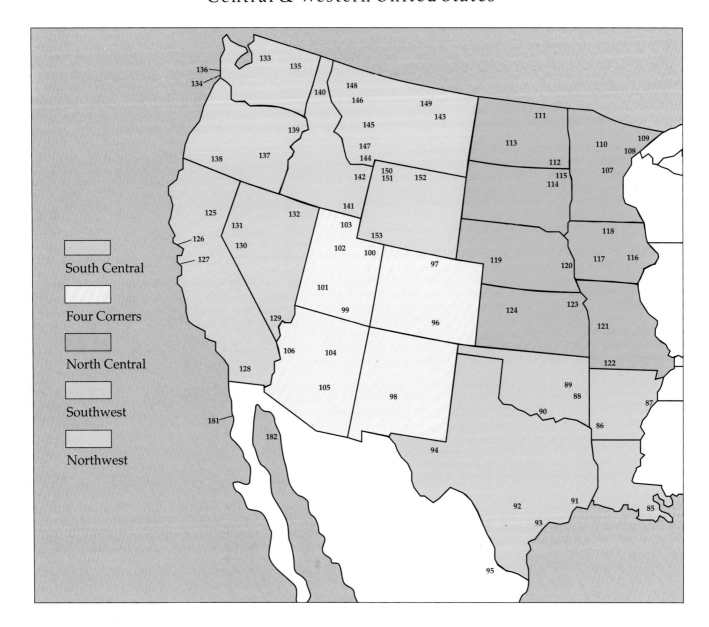

South Central

Four Corners

North Central

Southwest

Northwest

SOUTH CENTRAL UNITED STATES

State	Best Month(s)	Location
Louisiana	Oct.–May	85 Lake Pontchartrain
Arkansas	Sept.	86 Lake Millwood
	Feb.	87 Horseshoe Lake
Oklahoma	Apr., May, Nov.	88 Lake Tenkiller
	Apr., May, Nov., Dec.	89 Ft. Gibson Reservoir
	Nov., Dec.	90 Lake Texoma
Texas	Nov.–Mar.	91 Texas City dike
	Mar.	92 Lake O' The Pines
	Nov.–Mar.	93 Aransas Bay
	Mar.	94 Red Bluff Lake

EASTERN MEXICO

State	Best Month(s)	Location
Tamaulipas	Nov.–Mar.	95 Falcon Reservoir

FOUR CORNERS AREA—UNITED STATES

State	Best Month(s)	Location
Colorado	Nov. & Mar.	96 Pueblo Reservoir
	Apr., Oct., Nov.	97 Hamilton Reservoir
New Mexico	Apr., Oct., Nov.	98 Elephant Butte Reservoir
Utah	Apr., Oct., Nov.	99 Lake Powell
	Apr., Oct., Nov.	100 Steiner Reservoir
	Apr., Oct., Nov.	101 Minersville
	Apr., Oct., Nov.	102 Utah Lake
	Apr., Oct., Nov.	103 Bear Lake
Arizona	Apr., Oct., Nov.	104 Upper Lake Mary/ Ashurst Lake
	Apr., Oct., Nov.	105 Horseshoe Dam
	Apr., Oct., Nov.	106 Lake Havasu

NORTH CENTRAL UNITED STATES

State	Best Month(s)	Location
Minnesota	Apr., May, Oct., Nov.	107 Mille Lacs
	Nov., Dec	108 Duluth
	May–Sept.	109 Superior Nat. Forest
	May–Sept.	110 Chippewa Nat. Forest
North Dakota	May–Sept.	111 Turtle Mountains
	Apr., May, Oct., Nov.	112 Lake Tewaukon
	Apr., May, Oct., Nov.	113 Garrison Dam
South Dakota	Apr., May, Oct., Nov.	114 Waubay Lake
	Apr., May, Oct., Nov.	115 Mud Lake
Iowa	Apr., May, Oct., Nov.	116 Coralville Reservoir
	Apr., May, Oct., Nov.	117 Saylorville Reservoir
	Apr., May, Oct., Nov.	118 Clear Lake
Nebraska	Apr., May, Oct., Nov.	119 McConaughy Reservoir
	Apr., May, Oct., Nov.	120 Omaha

NORTH CENTRAL UNITED STATES *(continued)*

State	Best Month(s)	Location
Missouri	Apr., May, Oct., Nov.	121 Lake of the Ozarks
	Apr., May, Oct., Nov.	122 Table Rock Lake
Kansas	Apr., May, Oct., Nov.	123 Lake Perry
	Apr., May, Oct., Nov.	124 Cedar Bluffs Reservoir

SOUTHWEST UNITED STATES

State	Best Month(s)	Location
California	Apr.	125 Lake Almanor
	Apr. Oct.	126 Point Reyes
	Apr., May	127 Pigeon Point
	Apr.	128 Palomar Park
Nevada	Mar., Apr., Nov.	129 Lake Mead
	Apr., May, Nov.	130 Walker Lake
	May	131 Pyramid Lake
	May	132 Wild Horse Reservoir

NORTHWEST MEXICO

State	Best Month(s)	Location
Baja California Norte	Nov.–Mar.	181 San Quentin Bay
Sonora	Nov.–Mar.	182 Tiburon Island

NORTHWEST UNITED STATES

State	Best Month(s)	Location
Washington	Nov.	133 Lake Wenatchee
	Nov.–Mar.	134 Willapa NWR
	Apr.	135 Banks Lake
	Nov.–Mar.	136 Westport
Oregon	Oct., Nov.	137 Malheur Lake
	Sept.–Nov.	138 Upper Klamath Lake
	Oct., Nov	139 Wallowa Lake
Idaho	Sept.–Nov.	140 Coeur'd Alene Lake
	Apr., May	141 Twin Lakes Reservoir
	May–Sept.	142 Targhee Nat. Forest
Montana	Apr., May, Oct., Nov.	143 Ft. Peck Reservoir
	Apr., May, Oct., Nov.	144 Hebgen Lake
	Apr., May, Oct., Nov.	145 Canyon Ferry Reservoir
	Apr., May, Oct., Nov.	146 Flathead Lake
	Apr., May, Oct., Nov.	147 Ennis Lake
	May–Sept.	148 Flathead Nat. Forest
	Apr., May, Oct., Nov.	149 Nelson Reservoir
Wyoming	Apr., May	150 Squaw Lake, YNP
	May–Nov.	151 Yellowstone Lake, YNP
	Oct., Nov.	152 Lake DeSmet
	Apr., May, Oct., Nov.	153 Flaming Gorge Reservoir

Alaska & Canada

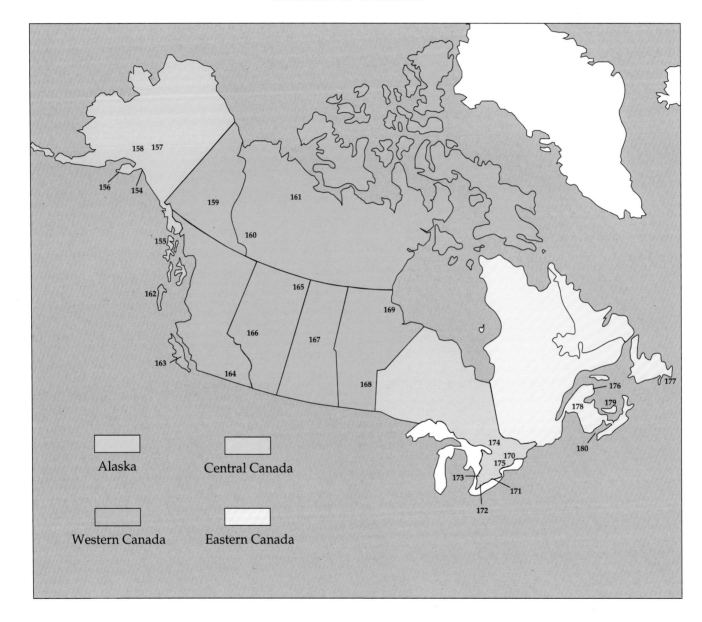

Alaska

Central Canada

Western Canada

Eastern Canada

ALASKA

State	Best Month(s)	Location
Alaska	Oct.–Mar.	154 Valdez
	Oct.–Mar.	155 Sitka
	May–Sept.	156 Kenai NWR
	May–Sept.	157 Minto Lake
	May–Sept.	158 Denali Nat. Park

CANADA

Province	Best Month(s)	Location

Western

Province	Best Month(s)	Location
Yukon	May–Sept.	159 Central Yukon
Northwest Territories	May–Sept.	160 Nahanni Nat. Park
	May– Sept.	161 Great Slave Lake
British Columbia	Nov.–May	162 Queen Charlotte Islands
	Nov.–May	163 Vancouver Island
	Apr.–Nov.	164 Okanagan Valley
Alberta	May–Sept.	165 Wood Buffalo Nat. Park
	May–Sept	166 Wabamun Lake
Saskatchewan	May–Sept.	167 Prince Albert Nat. Park
Manitoba	Apr.–Sept.	168 Lake Winnipeg
	May–Sept.	169 Churchill

Central

Province	Best Month(s)	Location
Ontario	Apr., May	170 Prince Edward Point
	Apr., May	171 Long Bird Point Observatory
	Apr., May, Oct., Nov.	172 Point Pelee
	Apr., May, Oct., Nov.	173 Sarnia/Kettle Point
	May–Oct.	174 Algonquin Prov. Park
	Apr., May	175 Toronto waterfront

Eastern

Province	Best Month(s)	Location
Quebec	Nov.–Mar.	176 Gaspé Peninsula
Newfoundland	Oct.–Apr.	177 St. Mary's Bay
New Brunswick	Oct.–Apr.	178 Miramichi Bay
Prince Edward Island	Oct.–Apr.	179 Malpeque Bay
Nova Scotia	Oct.–Apr.	180 Bay of Fundy

DESERT LOONS

I have read a number of articles on common loons, but one that caught my attention was an article describing how Hollywood was all wet. It went on to mention how one particular production that was filmed in the desert was technically wrong, because there was a common loon calling in the background. It insinuated that loons are not found in the desert.

I had just returned from an April trip to the southwestern United States and found common loons on numerous reservoirs in the desert. Not only that, but many of these birds were paired and in beautiful breeding plumage. These loons were migrating north. They were sort of out of place, considering typical loon habitat. When I heard the wailing calls of these loons echoing over the arid landscape, I realized common loon habitat is virtually any body of open water that is relatively undisturbed by people and has an ample supply of food. Given the right time of year, loons can be found almost anywhere in North America.

The Annual Life Cycle

Winter
The Molt

January is the beginning of a significant period in the annual cycle of the loon. During a typical winter, loons molt and seek out coastal areas that are relatively undisturbed by people and have an abundant supply of food. Beginning about the first week in January and extending to as late as mid-March (depending on the individual and the area), loons go through a flightless period. During this time of the year, the flight feathers are molted synchronously, rendering these birds completely flightless.

Synchronous molt is not restricted to loons; it occurs in ducks, geese, swans, anhingas, flamingos, pelicans, jacanas, auks, and grebes, as well. The molt is a stressful period for any bird and causes a tremendous energy drain. Birds lose a tremendous amount of body weight and counter this energy loss by consuming large amounts of food. The main function of the molt is to replace worn feathers; it is, in effect, a form of hygiene since it keeps the feathers in good condition. The worn feathers loosen in their follicles (where they are attached to the skin) and are pushed out of the follicles by the growing feathers beneath them.

During the molting period and throughout the winter months, loons spend most of their time feeding. Food is most often secured individually and is seldom if ever secured in groups. Wintering loons hold down individual feeding territories during daylight hours and return to groups, or rafts, only for nighttime protection. The length of feeding activity each day is a function of the amount of available daylight: as the amount of daylight increases, so does feeding activity. Loons typically begin feeding at dawn and stop feeding just before sunset.

Opposite: *In its never-ending pursuit of fish, a common loon is up with the sun.*

Common loons are aquatic predators. They are sight feeders and therefore require clear water and sunlight for stalking prey underwater. Wintering loons will secure a variety of food items depending on the time of year and the area. That loons feed on fish in the winter is well documented, but there is mounting evidence to suggest that arthropods play an important role as a food source for wintering loons in saltwater. Wintering loons in Rhode Island have been observed consuming small crabs, which are not only abundant and easy to swallow, but are also much easier to digest due to their relatively soft shells.

Loons stalk prey by peering, a method in which a loon cruises large areas by swimming the surface of the water. When a loon peers, it crouches its neck in an inverted **U** position and places its bill in the water with the eyes resting slightly below the waterline. Sometimes a loon can be observed moving its head slightly from side to side searching for prey underwater. Loons can cover tremendous distances stalking prey this way due to their extremely powerful legs.

Loons that winter along the coasts rely on the tides for both securing food and rafting for the night. Loons are most active in securing food during low and incoming tides. It is then that prey are most concentrated. Loons congregate for the night in deep open water areas along the coast.

A foraging adult peers underwater to spot prey.

When loons are not feeding, they are either preening or sleeping. Preening can include bathing as well as rubbing and scratching and helps alleviate itching while removing excess oil, dirt, and feather parasites. Feathers require a tremendous amount of care. Preening with oil from the uropygial gland occupies a good share of a loon's waking hours and serves as a natural form of waterproofing. It is accomplished when the loon's bill touches the oil gland located near the base of the tail. An oily fluid is then transferred to the feathers when the loon nibbles with its bill from the base to the tip of each feather. Hard-to-reach places, such as the cheeks and forehead, are taken care of by the foot touching the feathers. The neck is preened when laid against the feathers on the back and mantle. Feathers that have been preened in this manner give water repellency and buoyancy to loons, greatly adding to each bird's surface area while only minutely increasing its weight. The tips of these waterbird feathers are rough-textured and responsible for the water-repellent barrier that keeps buoyant air trapped underneath the belly feathers. Every square inch of the loon's plumage is preened on a daily basis.

Besides preening, loons spend a fair amount of time loafing and sleeping. Common loons, like a large number of birds, most often sleep very lightly. Many times they can be observed sleeping while their feet are moving. When nighttime sets in, loons congregate in loose flocks for protection. The typical sleeping posture has the head and neck draped over the back with the bill under the wing—the eyes are most often not obstructed by the wing. In fact, the eyes are very close to the wing and can easily be opened and closed to keep guard during sleep.

Loons can withstand a variety of temperature extremes, especially the cold. They are the only birds whose thighs are encased in skin, which provides additional insulation qualities to the thick layers of down and, depending on the season, large amounts of subcutaneous fat. Feathers add to the overall insulation properties of the loon's skin.

It is my belief that adult common loons pair-bond on the wintering areas as well as on the summer areas. This is a common occurrence with long-lived species such as cranes, swans, and eagles. Mated loon pairs must not winter far from one another. I base this on the fact that many loons arrive on the spring staging areas already pair-bonded. The first obvious signs of pair-bonding occur when loons acquire their breeding plumage, which usually occurs sometime in March. Don Skaar and I, in our studies of migrating loons in Montana and Wyoming, found most of these birds paired as they migrated north in April and May. This concurs with observations Mike Quinton and I have made of paired loons in the spring on reservoirs in southern Idaho, southern Wyoming, and northern Utah.

More specific information on wintering movements and behavior, staging, loon longevity, and population structures is unknown at this time. In order to get such data, loons have to be banded, color-marked, or even radio-tagged. The biggest obstacle to tagging is the lack of a capture technique. At the 1987 Conference on Common Loon Research and Management, held at Cornell University (Ithaca, NY), the topic of the development of a capture technique for common loons was discussed in detail. A capture technique should be developed within the next several years, but until that time, such aspects of loon behavior will remain a mystery.

A SPECIAL PLACE

One spring Mike Quinton visited a lake where loons usually nest to determine if the loons had arrived yet. He trudged through patches of snow and finally reached the lake. There in all its splendor was this beautiful lake, but it was missing one important component—the comon loon. Only about one-quarter mile of water was open on the lake at the time; the remainder was frozen. There was no sign of the loons.

Just as he was ready to leave, he noticed a loon far out in the skyline coming over the trees and circling the lake. Traveling several hundred yards in back of that loon was its mate. The loon pair soon landed on the small section of open water. They swam along the shore of the lake, and the female loon crawled up on a tiny island approximately three feet long. In a short period of time, the male also crawled up on the island and climbed on the back of the female. After copulation was complete, the male loon quickly dismounted and went back into the water and preened, while the female sat on the island for several seconds. She then entered the water and preened. Not long afterwards, the loon pair swam straight to the end of the open water, turned around and faced into the wind, and took off with feet pattering across the water. Finally airborne, the loons quickly disappeared over the lodgepole pine forest. The loons later returned and nested on the very same island, in the exact spot they had been observed copulating.

Early Spring
Migration and Pair-bonding

There are numerous signs when spring migration is about to occur. The days, of course, get longer, and temperatures get warmer. The loon's plumage changes as well: the dull gray feathers of winter are quickly replaced with new black and white feathers. The common loon magically changes from a wintering bird of ordinary beauty to a colorful springtime bird of uncommon beauty.

Besides the remarkable changes in physical appearance, loons become restless. The flight feathers at this point are close to reaching maximum growth and optimal feather condition known as hard-penned; there is little blood left in the primaries. Stretching exercises, such as wing-flapping and short practice flights over water, are constantly occurring. Small loose flocks soon turn into larger loose flocks, and vocalizations can be heard. Spring migration has begun.

Near the end of March, loons begin their spring-time migration and often congregate in staging areas where pair-bonding intensifies.

Near the end of March, common loons begin their springtime migration. This can involve traveling up the coast or through the interior of the continent—or both (Figure 6). Their arrival in an area is dependent on the temperature, which influences ice-out and the amount of open water available to loons. Migrant loons do most of their flying within the first three hours after sunrise. Their flight is distinguished by their fast wing beats (because of their short wings), low head, trailing legs, and hunched backs. They travel in loose flocks and often make their tremolo calls as they fly overhead. Since they have excellent eyesight, they often fly within sight of one another, which can be close, but is usually a considerable distance. Pairing and pair-bonding is strong by this time of the year. If ice-out is late in a particular area, loons congregate in the nearest open water, known as staging areas.

Staging areas are essential for migrant loons and not only provide safety and protection but also allow loons to advance farther north during migration. It is at these staging areas that pair-bonding intensifies, keeping the internal drive to nest alive. Residential adult territorial loons are the first to arrive in a nesting area, followed by migrants and floaters. Floaters are typically the nonbreeding segment of a population and are ready to pair-bond with another adult should a territory become available. The resident mated pairs arrive on staging areas and wait for their respective territories to open up. During spring migration, the male loon is the first to arrive in the area but is quickly followed by the female. At a typical staging area, loon pairs congregate in rafts only at night, and during the day feed within small individual territories of the larger staging area.

As the snow melts and more open water becomes available, loon pairs travel to satellite staging areas closer to the nesting territories. Paired loons leave the satellite staging areas often and fly out to check for ice-out. As the nesting territories gradually open up, loons leave the satellite staging area in pairs soon after dawn. Once the loons have left the staging area for the nesting territory, even if it is only partially open, they will not return to the staging area. They will remain in the nesting territory until fall. The internal drive to nest has begun.

*Large rafts of common loons form
in the evenings at the staging areas.*

Spring
Territoriality, Courtship, and Nesting

Once a breeding pair of loons have settled in on a lake, the serious business of defending the territory begins, whether it be for nesting, rearing chicks, or food. The size of a pair's territory varies from area to area, and no two territories are the same. There is a degree of flexibility to maintaining a territory, and adults have been known to leave their defended area for long lengths of time in search of food. On a small lake, the entire lake may be defended and is consequently a bona fide territory, whereas on larger lakes loon pairs defend only portions of the lake. Multiple pairs of breeding loons can coexist on larger lakes but the competition is extremely intense, especially with neighboring pairs and unmated individuals.

Loon courtship behavior is surprisingly quiet and subdued in comparison with other bird species.

Courtship is a more serious form of pair-bonding and occurs as soon as the loons arrive on the nesting territory in the spring. Loon courtship behavior is surprisingly quiet and subdued in comparison with other bird species. Subtle behavior such as swimming together, landing and taking off together, and mutual shallow dives are signs of courtship in full swing. The male loon is primarily responsible for stimulating the female to engage in copulation. The male will often climb up on the shoreline or on a small island and invite the female to follow. Communication at this time is coordinated with catlike meow calls made by either partner. The male usually goes through a few dry runs before the female accepts the invitation, but sometimes the female initiates the process by crawling up on land and enticing the male to follow. Precopulation behavior signs include the female laying down on land with her head slightly outstretched, facing straight ahead, with her bill pointing down, resembling the characteristic way a pelican holds its head. This signals the male to mount the female. The male then climbs and stands on the back of the female. The male lowers his head, faces forward, and lowers his rump (or vent) so there is cloacal contact with

the female. Then with a slight movement of the tail by the female, copulation occurs. The male quickly dismounts by sliding over the side or the head of the female and immediately enters the water. As with many birds, both sexes preen immediately after copulation. Copulation occurs quickly—in a matter of seconds—however, loons perform multiple copulations before and during nesting.

The area where the loons are seen copulating is most likely the area where they will nest; these nest sites will be used from year to year as long as they are not disturbed. Nest sites are always on the ground, preferably close to the mainland or close to larger islands.

Loon climbs out of nest, preparing to defend its territory.

In areas where significant lakeshore development has occurred, common loons will nest on artificial islands.

Quiet, secluded areas such as coves, backbays, and backwater areas are places where nests are typically found. However, there are exceptions: sometimes islands are not available for nesting, and loons must nest on the shoreline of a lake. Not all nesting sites are sheltered, but most offer some protection from the wind, for example the lee side of an island, promontory, or bay.

Common loons do not nest far from water because an incubating loon, while defending its nest, will slip into the water so the presence of the nest is undetected. Small masses of anchored vegetation, muskrat houses, and beaver lodges are used by nesting loons; loons will also nest on artificial islands, especially in areas where there is significant lakeshore development.

Both sexes are involved in nest building, however the female has the most contact with the nest. The nesting material consists mostly of arranged vegetation from the immediate vicinity, so nests tend to vary from place to place. Grasses, leaves, needles, mosses, roots, lake flotsam, and even submerged vegetation brought from the bottom of the lake can be used. I know of one loon nest in which the nest every year is comprised of a combination of submerged vegetation and large rusty nails. I have seen the loons carry these rusty nails in their bills to the nest site; they had to be getting them from the bottom of the lake.

After the loon pair goes through a series of copulations and a nest site has been selected, egg-laying begins. Common loon eggs are quite large—about the size of goose eggs. Their color is unique: olive green with a sprinkling of black and brown spots. (It should be noted that the common loon egg, because of its beauty, was prized by oologists [egg collectors] at the turn of the century. Today loon eggs are federally protected, thanks to laws such as the Migratory Bird Treaty Act of 1918.) There is a tremendous amount of color variation from egg to egg, especially from clutch to clutch. Where two eggs are laid in a clutch, the second egg is invariably smaller than the first. Common loons typically lay two eggs in a nest, although on rare occasions there may be three. If a loon nest is disturbed, a double clutch or a replacement clutch may occur, but this depends on the incubation stage of the previous clutch and whether or not the disturbance continues.

Loon on nest.

THE MISSING LOON EGG

One June I visited a loon nest in Wyoming and noticed from a distance that two eggs were in it. Two weeks later I visited the nest again and noticed there was only one egg remaining. It seemed to me that if predators were to blame, then both eggs would have been taken and there would be eggshell fragments present in the area, yet there was no sign of the missing egg at all.

In early July the single loon egg hatched, and I watched the loonlet riding on the back of one of the adults. I still wondered about the missing second egg, so I visited the nest in August, well after the loon family had left the area. I found no new clues.

I was in the same area again in September, so I decided to look one last time. The lake levels had dropped dramatically over the summer and were nearly three feet lower than the water levels had been in June. There, lying in six inches of water and twenty feet from the nest, was the missing egg. For some unexplained reason, the egg had rolled down into the water and managed to stay intact for over three months. How the egg got there is anyone's guess. One of the adults could have accidently rolled the egg off the nest trying to escape into the water, or high water levels in the spring could have washed the egg into the lake. Whatever the reason, I was glad to have solved the mystery of the missing egg.

Summer
Incubation, Territoriality, and Chick Development

The incubation period is a vulnerable time for common loons. Both adults share incubation duties and protect the eggs for a minimum of twenty-six days. During the partnership exchange of incubation duties, or during periods when a loon is forced to defend its nest, the eggs are left uncovered and exposed, leaving them vulnerable to weather and predation. Under normal circumstances, the adults leave the eggs exposed for only short periods of time when they exchange incubation duties. Weather-related activities such as floods, snow, and hail pose natural threats to incubating loons. High and low water levels are also serious threats to incubating loons because the nests, consisting of vegetation, normally rise with a rise in the water level. If there is too much of a rise in water level, the egg will likely flood out. Some loon nests can tolerate slight increases in water levels, but they are more the exception than the rule. I remember visiting one loon nest where the eggs were partially submerged in a quarter-inch of water, and I thought they were doomed. When I returned, I couldn't believe my eyes. The eggs had hatched, and the two loon chicks were riding on one parent's back. Low water levels can also be dangerous for incubating loons, since it leaves some nests high and dry. Because common loons have a difficult time walking on land, dry conditions can mean more time away from the nest, since there is a greater distance to travel between the shoreline and the nest; this leaves the eggs vulnerable to predation.

Adult broods on the nesting island.

Depending on the region, nest predators may include gulls, jaegers, ravens, crows, racoons, otters, skunks, weasels, minks, wolves, coyotes, and even bears. Humans, if they are not careful, can expose loon nests for long periods of time, thus making the eggs vulnerable to predators. A common loon brooding eggs has to put up with many annoyances, such as biting insects, rain, snow, hail, heat, and cold. Brooding loons are extremely attentive, keeping track of anything in the water, on the

land, and in the air. Sometimes they will even watch individual snow flakes fall to the ground, a fly buzzing overhead, or birds and airplanes flying over. If a bird flying overhead happens to be a predator, the brooding loon will sometimes crouch down and hide with its neck outstretched so its profile will not be detected. Common loons can also fall asleep brooding eggs. Signs of a loon sleeping on a nest include eyelids closed or starting to close, wings drooping over the nest, bill pointing up into the sky, and head tilted back.

Nest and loon veiled by the shadows of tall, emergent vegetation, which hides the nest.

Although incubation duties are shared by both adults, the female does most of the incubating. Besides providing protection and warmth to the eggs, a brooding loon must stand up and turn the eggs periodically in the most characteristic of all the nesting postures. The eggs are moved ever so slightly for good reason: the embryo in the egg is very delicate, so quick movement or jarring of the egg could kill the embryo; additionally, the eggs need to be turned periodically so that the embryo does not adhere to the shell and to keep the entire shell membrane moist and lubricated—an important component of a normal functioning egg. Incubating common loons do not have brood patches—an area in the belly region where there is no loss of feathers. According to loon experts, loons have an increased amount of blood vessels in that portion of the belly touching the eggs.

By the end of June and early July, common loon sounds have reached their peak. The male loon yodels quite often, announcing his individual territory, and in response, a male loon from a neighboring territory does the same. The sounds are incredible! Two resident male loons will face off where their territories adjoin one another and yodel at each other. The yodel is the most complex and longest of all the common loon calls. It also carries a tremendous amount of information, since each yodel identifies not only the caller but also emphasizes the mood

As hatching day approaches, loon wails increase in frequency and intensity.

of the calling loon. A yodel consists of an introduction, identifying the individual male loon, followed by a phrase a loon repeats a number of times. A few repeats indicate the bird is angry, but continual repeats indicate the loon is severely agitated. The wail, which sounds like a howling coyote or wolf, is the call most commonly associated with the common loon. The wail also reaches its peak just before the loon chicks hatch and is always the predominant nighttime chorus. Both loons will wail together at night, and if more than one pair gets in on the action, a symphony of sounds fill the air. The incredible chorus is a clear indication the chicks will soon hatch.

The first indication that a chick is about to hatch comes from the behavior of the brooding adult, who will stare down at its breast and twitch ever so slightly, telescoping a behavioral message that a chick is starting to pip, or crack, the eggshell. Even before the chick hatches, there is communication between the brooding adult and the large active embryo inside the egg. The communication is difficult to describe, but the adult makes noises such as clicks and groans similar to the sounds made by chickens. This communication also occurs while the chick is pipping the egg and immediately after hatching. Chicks, whether they are still pipping the egg or several days old, make a peeping call in communicating with the adults. As the chick first cracks a hole in the egg, a tiny white pointed egg tooth, used to crack the eggshell, can be easily seen on the upper tip of the bill. This egg tooth will disappear by the time the chick is approximately one month old.

One of the first signs that an egg is about to hatch is the brooding adult raising up slightly to check the egg.

Opposite: *Day-old loon chick and pipping egg.* Left: *Newly hatched chick is protected under the adult's wing.*

The chick hatches from the egg within twenty-four hours of first cracking the egg. If another egg is present, it will usually hatch within twenty-four hours of the first hatched chick. Signs that a chick has hatched include the brooding adult lifting its wing ever so slightly, especially near the tips of the wing. This is in anticipation of the chick wanting to crawl underneath the wing. After each chick has hatched, one of the adults carries off in its bill the egg membrane with attached pieces of eggshell and sinks it into deep water. By doing so, it is believed, predators will not be attracted to the nest. When first out of the shell, the chicks are wet. They dry off within a few hours after hatching through a combination of the sun's warmth, their own body heat, and warmth from the feathers of the adult. From a distance, the chicks appear to be completely black, but they do have white bellies. Loon

Chicks ride on the adult's back to travel, rest, escape danger, and keep warm.

chicks have surprisingly large and well-developed feet, especially after hatching. Such large feet allow the chicks to be mobile. Newly hatched chicks are full of energy, climbing under and over the brooding adults. If they accidently fall off an adult to the ground they are cushioned from injury by the dense natal down. This same down is so thick that it repells water and keeps the chick afloat, thus acting as a natural life preserver.

The chicks soon become hungry after emerging from the eggs. The adults coax the chicks to leave the small nest and enter the water, where they are immediately fed small aquatic insects. Chick feeding and resting is fairly well restricted at this time to sheltered coves and backbay areas. Chicks quickly learn to climb on the back of the adult.

The adult facilitates this process by slightly submerging the body, allowing the chicks to climb on board. Chicks ride on the back of the adults for a number of reasons, including warmth, traveling, resting, and escaping danger. I remember watching a small loon chick ride on the back of an adult. The wind had come up and the water was extremely choppy. The lone chick actually held on to the back of the adult's neck with its small bill so it would not fall off. Mike Quinton has seen adults carrying day-old chicks on their backs, lifting and raising one wing then another as they are swimming to keep the chick from tumbling into the water.

Loon chick rides under a parent's wing through the lily pads.

When the loon chicks are very small, it is important that the adults make the chicks follow them. By doing so, the chicks quickly imprint on the adults. This imprinting behavior is also apparent in ducks, geese, and cranes, and is a way of strengthening the family bond, which is important for survival. Ideal areas for rearing chicks usually include two important elements: a quiet sheltered nursery area and an adequate supply of small food. The young chicks swim behind the parents to the nursery area and will often alternate by following one parent and then another leaving what is called a zigzag pattern. They stay in small nursery areas for the first couple of weeks, but the size of the nursery areas actually expands as the chicks become older.

The loonlets are fed primarily small fish, but depending on the circumstances they will also eat aquatic insects, leeches, salamanders, frogs, crayfish, and aquatic vegetation. Up until the time the loonlets are a few days old, a typical feeding scenario involves one adult diving for food while the other adult stays on the surface with the young. When the diving adult surfaces with food, it will go directly to the chick and feed it. The adult offering the food can either exchange the food directly from its bill to the chick's bill or drop the fish and pick it up, as though the fish were still alive. This is an important lesson for the chick since common loons feed primarily on live prey.

The chick eagerly rushes to its parent, who has emerged with a small insect larva.

The carefully reared chicks develop quite rapidly and become more independent as the days pass. The female loon stays with the chicks continuously for the first two weeks. Changes in their plumage are signs that the chicks are developing fast. By two weeks, the chicks appear to be more brown than black and are one-quarter the size of the adults. By three or more weeks, they will swim to the adults for food, and back-riding is almost nonexistent. During this period of development, the small chicks remain on the surface of the water while the adults dive in search of food. The adults continuously drop food in the water by the time the chicks are four weeks old, thus encouraging them to capture moving prey. At approximately four weeks of age, the chicks change into a brown juvenal plumage and become more independent. Time is of the essence if the loonlet is going to successfully fledge and migrate.

The female loon stays with the chick continuously for the first two weeks after its hatching.

LOON DEFENSE

Common loons are very protective of their nesting territory. Mike Quinton once observed two trumpeter swans landing on a lake where there were nesting loons. The adult swans swam around the lake together, cruising the shoreline and covering a large amount of area. When they came within twenty yards of an incubating loon on its nest island, problems began for the swans. The male loon appeared from nowhere and trailed one hundred feet behind the trumpeter swans. The male loon's neck was outstretched and low to the water, resembling a surfacing submarine. It was as if the submarine were keeping track of two large aircraft carriers (the swans). The agitated loon would dive under the swans and stab at them. The swans would tread water to keep the aggressive loon away; the swans sensed the danger and quickly swam out of that area.

Above water there was no obvious attack on the swans by the loon, but the defender was determined to pester the intruders until they left the area. Maybe such defenses have to do with the size of the intruder and the perceived threat. On small lakes, common loons have a tendency to chase all small- to medium-sized waterfowl off nesting lakes. Common loons will dive and splash at ducks until they leave the immediate area. Larger birds such as sandhill cranes appear to be no threat as they fly over the territories, but raptors such as ospreys and bald eagles cause loons great concern. Male common loons defending nesting territories will even yodel when they see low-flying airplanes. Adult territorial loons will defend an area if the threat is perceived to be real, regardless of the size of the intruder.

Autumn
Chick Fledging and Migration

When loonlets are nine to eleven weeks of age, they continually practice flying. The most common exercise is the wing stretch, where they paddle their feet, get up on their rump, and stretch their wings. They also practice short flights, which are often followed by crash landings. By the time the loonlets are eleven to twelve weeks old, they are able to fly and their juvenal plumage is more gray than brown. The loonlets have high activity levels and are constantly practicing flying, diving, splashing, and wailing. As the days progress, the adults leave the nesting territory for longer periods of time until one day they do not return and the loonlets are on their own. The wildlife activity around the lake dies down tremendously. Food is not as easily available, and there is thick frost on the grass and ice forming on the edge of the lake in the mornings. Migrant loons can be seen flying over the lake, heading south. It is time for the juvenile loons to leave.

The wing stretch is a common exercise for loonlets learning to fly.

The juvenile loons quickly begin investigating unfamiliar areas or lakes. The biological clock of the loon, based on environmental conditions, urges it to migrate. The study of migration is not an exact science; there is so much that is not known. The temperature, photoperiod, position of the sun, earth's magnetic field, and natural guiding lines are all instrumental in assisting migrating loons. For the common loon, the typical migration months are September through November, with the bulk of the autumn migration occurring in September and October, especially in the northern latitudes and at high elevations. Migrant loons begin congregating on staging areas during the day. When some of these staging areas start freezing over, migrant loons then congregate on larger lakes that are free of ice. Migrants can be singled out on these lakes because they are normally found in deep water areas where one rarely observes foraging loons.

The change in environmental conditions becomes more complex and presents constant choices as loons migrate south from one area to another. Loons migrate during the day and follow routes or corridors used by other waterfowl; they use traditional natural guiding lines such as rivers, lakes, valleys, and mountain ranges for orientation. However, loon migration is not restricted to corridors but can be overland, as well. After migrating to the next lake or reservoir, their length of stay in an area depends on environmental conditions, undisturbed places for nesting, and clear water areas with an adequate supply of food.

Since loon migration information is very limited, information on their arrival at coastal wintering areas is based on personal observations. Common loons arrive on the Florida coast anywhere from the third week in October to the second week in November. Not all common loons winter on the coast, however. Some will winter in the interior of the continent on lakes and reservoirs that are ice-free. The Great Lakes region and the Southwest deserts are areas where common loons can be found in the winter. But for the majority of common loons, the coastal areas provide optimal winter habitat.

Fall migration typically occurs from September through November, and the loons will gradually undergo their seasonal plumage change.

Winter
Congregating Again

December. Most of the loons found congregating along the coast have been there for over a month. The adults' plumage looks ragged, and the juveniles look about the same as they did in autumn when they acquired their new feathers. The molting subadults and adults are in for a long physiologically stressful period known as the molt.

The coastal winter habitat is completely different from the inland lakes where many of the loons raised their young. The water environment has changed from fresh- to saltwater. Oceans and coastal areas are extremely complex and dynamic. The tides are pulses of the living ocean that make available to loons a variety of food items. Common loons have a number of obstacles to overcome if they are to survive the winter on the ocean. Environmental extremes such as hurricanes, blizzards, storms, and cold temperatures can be taxing on a molting loon. There are also human-induced hazards such as fishing nets, environmental contaminants, and collisions with wires. All play an important role in the overall survival of wintering common loons, but the prospects for survival are great.

Not all loons migrate for the winter; some stay on inland lakes, particularly during mild winters.

As the common loon returns to the ocean, the annual cycle is complete. For the time being, this phantom of the water will be relatively quiet and dull-colored. In less than five months, this bird will be on its way again, in its most splendid of colors, migrating north to nest and raise young. The thrilling wild sounds will return to the northern lakes.

Epilogue
Loons as Environmental Indicators

"When the last individual of a race of living things breathes no more, another heaven and earth must pass before such a one can be again."

In the words of Charles Kuralt, "the only thing constant about man is change." Monitoring environmental quality values and wilderness values will require monitoring change. Grizzly bear expert and naturalist John Craighead most eloquently captures the importance of wilderness and wilderness areas, by stating: "They are laboratories destined to become environmental monadnocks in an age of progressive world environmental change.... They serve as benchmarks by which to measure and evaluate future massive, man-caused environmental alterations in our non-wilderness habitat."

Common loons are the barometers of a quality environment. Monitoring these feathered "environmental monadnocks" can be a way of monitoring the seriousness of human-induced environmental changes caused by acid rain, air pollution, water pollution, nuclear waste, toxic chemicals, and outdoor recreation, to name a few. Not all these environmental changes are localized: some are global in scope. By monitoring common loon numbers and/or reproduction, we are in fact indirectly monitoring human-induced change. Since loons are on top of the aquatic food chain, a negative change in their well-being may be an indication that something is wrong with the environment. As a wildlife biologist, I have always held to the slogan, "You can only manage on what you know." Having good information about a particular species is the best means of managing that species. The key to managing wildlife is to manage people; the best way of managing people is by slowing down life's pace in a conscientious and responsible manner.

The earth is no longer a wildlife world with people in it, but is today a people world with wildlife in it. The human population is expanding, placing increased pressure on the earth's natural resources and the natural environment. There is only one way to slow the rate at which our resources are being expended: conservation is the wise use

of our resources, whether they be natural or synthetic. If we are to have wildlife and wild places for the future, we must learn to conserve in our everyday lives. We need to insist on energy conservation and recycling. If we use our resources wisely, in a conscientious and responsible manner, all species will benefit, especially the common loon.

Naturalist William Beebe once wrote: "When the last individual of a race of living things breathes no more, another heaven and earth must pass before such a one can be again." These words emphasize the idea of extinction of any species. If we use our resources wisely, there is hope for common loons and other species; if there is hope for other species, there is hope for us.

There are many things that private citizens can do to make our environment harmonious for people and common loons. If you really do love loons and care about their welfare, there is no organization quite like the North American Loon Fund. As a professional wildlife biologist, I can attest that of all the organizations I have had contact with in my career, very few come close to the NALF. Their practical approach to wildlife management, their positive attitude, and the camaraderie of the members make it a one-of-a-kind organization. If you enjoy loons and you want to get involved, join the NALF, by contacting:

North American Loon Fund
RR 4 Box 240C
High Street
Meredith, New Hampshire 03253
Tel. (603) 279-6163

Another organization I respect is The Nature Conservancy. Some natural or wild areas need to be saved specifically for wildlife. If you want to contribute to a great cause by preserving wildlife habitat, try contacting:

The Nature Conservancy
1815 North Lynn Street
Arlington, Virginia 22209
Tel. (703) 841-5300

Get to know the common loons in your area. Wintering and staging areas for common loons are just as important as nesting areas. Take an active part in doing something for loons. Please give loons the space they need. If conditions warrant, build an artificial nest structure, educate the public, become a loon ranger on a lake or coastal shoreline. Think positive! Nothing is more gratifying than doing something to benefit the common loon.

Appendix

There are undoubtedly hundreds of people who have been instrumental in preserving loon habitat and, consequently, loon populations in this country and abroad, but there are eight individuals whose efforts on behalf of the common loon, I believe, deserve mention. They have devoted most of their lives to loon preservation, and I would therefore like to commend their efforts here, if only briefly.

William Barklow has been involved with the North American Loon Fund for over twenty years, and his most significant contribution has been in the area of recording loon vocalizations. Written and produced by Barklow, *Voices of the Loon* was made possible by funding from the National Audubon Society and was the driving force behind the establishment of the North American Loon Fund as a full-fledged conservation organization. The record is a monumental breakthrough in educating the public about the common loon.

Herb Cilley, to whom this book is dedicated, is known in New Hampshire as the loon man and the loon ranger. The loons of Bow Lake became part of his family, so to speak, and recognize Cilley well enough to allow him within five feet of them. His reputation for being one of the best loon rangers ever is well deserved, for he has been instrumental in educating the residents and visitors of Bow Lake about the common loon and in garnering respect for them. When new boaters get too close to nesting loons, Herb educates them by giving them an entertaining lecture and picture postcards of the birds. He is an outspoken educator and loon advocate, a self-taught ornithologist, who epitomizes what one individual can do to help protect local threatened species.

Jeff Fair is currently the director of the New Hampshire Loon Preservation Committee. His accomplishments are plenty, but he takes great pride in his grassroots approach to loon conservation. The biggest accomplishment of the NHLPC has been the successful negotiation of workable agreements with hydroelectric authorities in managing lake water levels. This benefits not only loons, but recreationists as well. His efforts to encourage volunteer support for the organization have proven highly successful, and he believes such one-on-one relationships with individual wildlife species and their environment are the keys to habitat and species preservation.

Judith McIntyre is currently a professor of biology at Utica College of Syracuse University and has earned the nickname loon lady because of her ongoing dedication to the common loon. She has studied them for twenty-two years all across the North American continent, and in 1971 initiated a program in Minnesota known as Project Loon Watch. Many of her findings have been published, including a 1989 article in *National Geographic* entitled "The Common Loon Cries for Help."

Don Skaar is a third-generation biologist whose father, Dave Skaar, was the first to study Montana loons in depth. Don decided to keep his father's legacy going, so he took over the chores of monitoring common loons in Montana for the North American Loon Fund in 1983. He believes that loons, because of their charm and appeal, are most effective in helping people become aware of all wildlife. The concern for common loons, he argues, will create a domino effect and actually help in the conservation not only of loons but of all wildlife.

Paul Strong appeared on Mutual of Omaha's "Wild Kingdom" in 1982, which featured the common loons on Paul's study area in Maine. This film won an award for the best animal behavior film at the annual International Wildlife Film Festival. Strong has been actively involved in the North American Loon Fund since 1985, with his activities ranging from trustee, to director of programs, to editor of the proceedings from the 1987 Conference on Loon Research and Management. He is currently a wildlife ecologist working for the U.S. Forest Service in Minnesota.

Scott Sutcliffe worked as a youth counselor at a hiking and canoe-ing camp on Squam Lake in New Hampshire during his college years, and after college secured a job with the Squam Lake Association, which was looking for someone to study common loons. Sutcliffe conducted the first statewide common loon census, became the first director of the New Hampshire Loon Preservation Committee, and organized the first loon festival in New Hampshire. He discovered that power boats were not the primary cause of a declining loon population on the lake, but that canoeists and fishermen were the primary culprits. In the late 1970s, Sutcliffe became the first director of the newly organized North American Loon Fund. Since NALF, Sutcliffe has worked for The Nature Conservancy in New York and is currently the associate director of the Cornell Lab of Ornithology.

Rawson Wood is indeed the father of the loon preservation move-ment. He has had an abiding interest in common loons since 1943 when he managed to record loon calls during a visit to Elk Lake in the Adirondacks. He has been chairman of the loon committee of the New Hampshire Audubon Society, a post he held for fourteen years, and was chairman of the Squam Lake Association, which conducted the first loon census. This resulted in a statewide loon survey, which compared recent with historical loon nesting statistics. The most significant find-ing was that common loons had disappeared from one-half of the lakes that they historically occupied. Through great efforts, Wood helped in getting the common loon placed on the New Hampshire threatened species list, and a chain reaction started in neighboring states. Ulti-mately, the North American Loon Fund was founded and today boasts hundreds of members and over a dozen affiliates.

Squam Lake, incidentally, was the setting for the movie *On Golden Pond,* which starred the Squam Lake common loons and in which Rawson served as technical consultant.

Glossary

Adult: term for a bird that is in final plumage; even though some bird species can breed or nest when they are in immature or subadult plumage, they are not classified as an adult until they reach the plumage of a breeding adult.

Breeding plumage: also called alternate plumage, most commonly recognized black and white adult summer plumage.

Fingerprint: feathers on the side of the neck of an adult common loon in breeding/alternate plumage; black and white necklace feathers identifying individual loons.

Immature: a young bird during either its first year or a series of years before it acquires its adult plumage. In common loons, the immature plumage lasts longer than one year and can extend up to three years in some individuals.

Juvenal: the plumage associated with a newly hatched chick.

Juvenile: a young bird that moves freely on its own, but has yet to complete its post-juvenal molt.

Lantern: the breast of an adult common loon in breeding/alternate plumage.

Loonlet: a loon chick, a juvenile, or immature loon.

Molt: the periodic replacement of feathers; the shedding or loss of old feathers followed by the replacement and growth of new feathers.

Monadnock: a hill or mountain of resistant rock surrounded by a peneplain; a mountain that stands alone.

Necklace: black and white feathers found on both the throat and the neck of an adult common loon in breeding or alternate plumage; this includes the throat patch.

Paragon: a model.

Primaries: the main flight feathers of the wing, usually attached to the "hand" portion of the wing. Common loons have eleven primaries on each wing.

Remiges: flight feathers; wing feathers consisting of primaries and secondaries. Common loons have thirty-three to thirty-four remiges (primaries and secondaries) on each wing, depending on the individual.

Retrices: tail feathers. Common loons have sixteen to twenty retrices, depending on the individual.

Secondaries: secondary flight feathers of the wing attached to the forearm. Common loons have twenty-two to twenty-three secondaries on each wing, depending on the individual.

Throat patch: the series of small vertical white feathers found on the throat of a common loon in breeding plumage; part of the necklace.

Uropygial gland: preen gland located at the base of the tail.

Winter plumage: also called basic plumage, most commonly recognized by brown and/or gray-colored feathers.

Bibliography

Alexander, L. L. 1987. Patterns of mortality in wintering Common Loons. In *Papers from the 1987 Conference on Loon Research & Management,* ed. P. Strong, 77. Meredith, New Hampshire: North American Loon Fund.

Barklow, W. 1990. The haunting songs of the north. *Wildlife Conservation* 93, no. 2 (March-April): 46–59.

Barr, J. F. 1973. Feeding biology of the Common Loon (*Gavia immer*) in oligotrophic lakes of the Canadian shield. Ph.D. diss., University of Guelph, Ontario.

Bellrose, F. C. 1980. *Ducks, geese, and swans of North America.* Washington, D. C.: Wildlife Management Institute; Harrisburg, Pennsylvania: Stackpole Books.

Bent, A. C. 1919. *Life histories of North American diving birds.* Smithsonian Institution, U. S. Natural History Museum, Bulletin 107. Washington, D. C.: U. S. Government Printing Office.

Christoff, M. 1979. Study of the early chick rearing period of the Common Loon (*Gavia immer*). SUNY College of Environmental Science and Forestry. Typescript.

Craighead, J. J., J. S. Sumner, and G. B. Scaggs. 1982. *A definitive system for analysis of Grizzly Bear habitat and other wilderness resources—utilizing LANDSAT multispectral imagery and computer technology.* Wildlife-Wildlands Institute Monograph no. 1. Missoula: Univ. of Montana.

Daub, B. C. 1987. Behavior of Common Loons in winter. In *Papers from the 1987 Conference on Loon Research & Management,* ed. P. Strong, 117. Meredith, New Hampshire: North American Loon Fund.

Dement'ev, G. P. et al. 1968. *Birds of the Soviet Union.* Translated from Israel Program for Scientific Translations, Vol. 2. Moscow, U. S. S. R.; Jerusalem, Israel.

Dunning, J. 1986. *The Loon—Voice of the wilderness.* Dublin, New Hampshire: Yankee Books.

Gabrielson, I. N. 1959. *Birds of Alaska.* Harrisburg, Pennsylvania: Stackpole Books.

Harrison, C. 1982. *An atlas of the birds of the Western Palaearctic.* Princeton, New Jersey: Princeton Univ. Press.

Howell, A. H. 1932. *Florida bird life.* New York: Coward-McCann, Inc.

Janssen, R. B. 1987. *Minnesota birds.* Minneapolis: Univ. of Minn. Press.

Kennedy, R. J. 1972. The probable function of flexules. *Ibis* 114:265–266.

Klein, T. 1985. *Loon magic.* Ashland, Wisconsin: Paperbirch Press, Inc.

Linsdale, J. M. 1936. *Birds of Nevada.* Berkeley, California: Cooper Ornith. Club.

112 Lowery, G. H., Jr. 1955. *Louisiana birds.* Baton Rouge: Louisiana State Univ. Press.

McIntyre, J. W. 1978. Wintering behavior of the Common Loon. *Auk* 95: 183–186.

———————— 1988. *The Common Loon—Spirit of northern lakes.* Minneapolis: Univ. of Minnesota Press.

———————— 1989. The Common Loon cries for help. *National Geographic,* April, 510–524.

Oberholser, H. C. 1974. *The bird life of Texas.* Vol. 1. Austin: Univ. of Texas Press.

Palmer, R. S. 1962. *Handbook of North American birds.* Vol. 1. New Haven, Connecticut: Yale University Press.

Pearson, T. G. 1942. *Birds of North Carolina.* Raleigh, North Carolina: Bynum Printing.

Powers, K. D. and J. Cherry. 1983. Loon migrations off the northeastern United States. *Wilson Bulletin* 95: 125–132.

Salo, L. J. 1975. *A baseline survey of significant marine birds in Washington State.* Coastal Zone Environmental Studies Report No. 1. Olympia: Washington Dept. of Game.

Skaar, D. and T. P. McEneaney. 1988. Timing and structure of the migrating Common Loon population in Montana during 1988. North American Loon Fund. Typescript.

Strong, P. I. 1985. Habitat selection by Common Loons. Ph.D. diss., Univ. of Maine, Orono.

———————— 1987. *Papers from the 1987 Conference on Loon Research & Management.* Meredith, New Hampshire: North American Loon Fund.

Sutcliffe, S. A. 1980. Aspects of the nesting ecology of Common Loons in New Hampshire. Master's thesis, Univ. of New Hampshire, Durham.

Yonge, K. S. 1981. The breeding cycle and annual production of the Common Loon (*Gavia immer*) in the boreal forest region. Master's thesis, Univ. of Manitoba, Winnipeg.

Zimmer, K. J. 1985. *The western bird watcher.* Englewood Cliffs, New Jersey: Prentice-Hall Inc.